"In this age when overpromising and underdelivering are commonplace, there is one promise that will deliver: praying for your marriage will enrich, enhance, and fortify your life, marriage, and family. In his book *Pray Big for Your Marriage*, Will Davis provides you with the tools needed to develop a powerful prayer life for your marriage. Whether you've been married fifty years or fifty days, you need to read and apply the principles in this book."

Dennis Rainey, president and cofounder, FamilyLife

"Will Davis demonstrates why prayer should be a nonnegotiable ingredient for a thriving relationship. This book will help couples not only survive marriage but also take it to a higher level. As a marriage counselor, I would have to say this will be required reading!"

Dr. Samuel Adams, coauthor, *The Ten Commandments of Dating* and *Devotions for Dating Couples*

"In *Pray Big for Your Marriage*, Will Davis has written a gem of a book. Anyone who wants a successful, healthy marriage should read this book. I wish it had been available early on in my marriage. There is no greater gift a husband and wife can give each other than to pray together. Will understands that and helps guide couples through that process with this insightful and compelling book."

Rick Johnson, founder, Better Dads; author, *That's My Son*

"Will Davis has become a regular on my radio program, and I am honored to call him my friend and brother. Will reminds us that God is going to paint our lives with brilliant colors as we pray big, when we ask him to make our marriages into what he wants them to be—satisfying and full of life. Thank you, Will, for teaching us to ask God—to trust God—to make our marriages into his vision of what they should be!"

Nancy Turner, host, *This Is The Day!*
WMBI FM Moody Radio, Chicago

"As a marriage and family therapist, I cannot stress strongly enough the importance of praying for your marriage, but most couples don't even know where to start. This book provides a much-needed road map for those couples who would like to enhance the power of prayer in their marriage."

Rick Reynolds, LCSW, founder, Affair Recovery Center

"*Pray Big for Your Marriage* reflects Will's personality—challenging yet compassionate, brutally honest yet tactful, intense yet playful. I have watched Will for twenty-five-plus years, and he knows how to pray. His book specifically challenged me in a *big* way—to pray without ceasing as I relentlessly love my wife."

Byron Weathersbee, EdD, Legacy Family Ministries

PRAY BIG

for Your

MARRIAGE

The Power of Praying God's Promises
for Your Relationship

WILL DAVIS JR.

Revell

a division of Baker Publishing Group
Grand Rapids, Michigan

© 2008 by Will Davis Jr.

Published by Revell
a division of Baker Publishing Group
P.O. Box 6287, Grand Rapids, MI 49516-6287
www.revellbooks.com

Printed in the United States of America

Library of Congress Cataloging-in-Publication Data
Davis, Will, 1962–
      Pray big for your marriage : the power of praying God's promises for your
   relationship / Will Davis, Jr.
        p.   cm.
      Includes bibliographical references.
      ISBN 978-0-8007-3245-5 (pbk.)
        1. Marriage—Religious aspects—Christianity. 2. Prayer—Christianity.
   I. Title.
   BV835.D387 2008
   248.3′208655—dc22   2008000343

09   10   11   12   13   14   15   9   8   7   6   5   4

To my loving wife, Susie.
No person has prayed for me more.
No person has needed to.

CONTENTS

ACKNOWLEDGMENTS

Susie—You are a godly woman, a wonderful wife, my partner in ministry, and my closest friend. Proverbs 31:10 asks, "A wife of noble character who can find?" I did.

Will III, Emily, and Sara—You each amaze and inspire me. Thanks for making my job as a dad so easy. I couldn't be more proud of you.

My dad, Will D. Davis—You are the best example of a serving husband I've ever seen. Thanks for being such a great role model.

Vicki Crumpton—Thank you for going to bat for me and for supporting *Pray Big* and *Pray Big for Your Marriage*. Your input and encouragement have been invaluable. Thanks for great coaching on the testosterone-free chapter.

Suzie Cross—You have become a friend, albeit a long-distance one. Thanks for your tireless efforts to make *Pray Big* and *Pray Big for Your Marriage* successful. You are a joy to work with and a great example of a true prayer warrior.

Jessica Miles—Thanks for using your impeccable editing skills to make *Pray Big* and *Pray Big for Your Marriage* easier to read. And thanks for being patient with me!

Brooke Nolen, Claudia Marsh, and Deonne Beron—Thank you for your excellent work in marketing *Pray Big*.

Les Stobbe—You are a mighty man of God. I love your heart and passion for the gospel. Thanks for great advice, encouragement, and friendship.

Terri Crow—You have amazing proofreading skills. Thank you for your generous, consistent, and cheerful contributions to this work.

Wendy Browning—You are a wonderful assistant and a ruthless proofreader! Thanks for being such a fun co-worker and friend.

Tonya Parrott—Dr. Parrott, I presume. You have been a joy to get to know. I love what God is doing in the lives of you and your family. Thanks for supporting me and for your excellent work on this book.

Lori Howe—You are a true friend. Thanks for reading the text and for offering candid advice: "Will, you didn't tell me how to pray for my marriage!"

Gary and Jackie Sinclair—I'm so glad you became Texans! Thanks for being godly examples of a Christian marriage. Gary, thanks also for your proofing and helpful comments.

Andrea Smith—God sent an angel to Will and Susie, and her name was Andrea. . . . Thanks for loving us, believing in us, and supporting us. You have been a huge encouragement to Susie and me.

David Washington—Thanks for being a godly man, a good friend, and a great example of a serving husband.

Ryan and Courtney Nowakowski—I'm so proud of you both. Thanks for having a kingdom marriage. Austin Christian Fellowship (ACF) is a healthier church because of your obedience.

Alan and Tina Nagel—Thanks for believing in ACF and for adding credibility to our cause. Thank you for obeying God's call and for impacting countless lives over the decades. Alan, thank you for being a great advisor, friend, and mentor. Tina, thank you for dreaming of a kingdom church.

Rick and Stephanie Reynolds—I love you both. Rick, thanks for being my friend and for keeping me in the kingdom game. Thanks to you both for fighting for marriages. You are true kingdom heroes.

John and Helen Boyd—Johnny, thanks for knocking on my door. Thanks to you both for having a marriage that changes lives.

Brandon and Amber Parker—I'm so thrilled that God brought you into my life. You inspire me and make me want to be a better Christian.

ACF overseers, board of directors, and staff—I love each of you. I love being in community with you and serving our King together. Thanks for putting up with me.

1

DEARLY BELOVED . . . PRAY!

RECENTLY MY WIFE, Susie, and I had the opportunity to fly out to beautiful Southern California from our home in Austin. We went there to film six DVD lessons for a curriculum on marriage we were writing for our church.

It was an exciting experience for both of us. Susie and I are not experts on marriage. We would be the first to tell you that we know as much about what *not* to do in marriage as what *to* do. But because I am the senior pastor of our church and Susie is my wife, somewhere in those roles we get tagged as having something to say about marriage. And since the trip was free and included some fun downtime, we figured we'd give the DVD thing a shot.

We spent about six hours in a Los Angeles studio, being directed by two of the most talented Christian media and curriculum producers in the country. The sessions went well, and the producers seemed pleased with the end product. Afterward we drove over to the Ritz Carlton in Dana Point and treated ourselves to a romantic dinner, complete with candles and a 180-degree view of the Pacific. Over dinner we talked about how blessed we were even to be in a position to talk about marriage to others. We reflected on the day and how much fun we'd had. On the thirty-minute drive back to our hotel, we held hands and continued to list God's great blessings in our lives. It was a perfect evening.

Until I got lost.

Actually, Susie thought I was lost. I viewed myself as just a little "off course." Now, if you're a woman, your husband is driving, you're in a strange area a thousand miles from home, and it's totally dark outside, then the difference between "lost" and "off course" is a moot point.

Susie first got suspicious when the scenery began to change. Our hotel was in a well-developed urban area—lights, intersections, Home Depots, and Starbucks. You know—friendly, comforting, and familiar landmarks that signal civilization. But the scenery on our drive back was ... well, scenery—trees, open fields, livestock, wild animals, and narrow, semipaved roads with a streetlight every fifteen miles. It was pretty obvious to Susie that, while we were *somewhere*, we weren't near where we were supposed to be. It was also obvious that I had no clue where we were.

The great news about being lost in the country is that, if you're looking for the city, all you have to do is aim for the lights. So we did. And after a quick, alarm-sounding drive through a tollbooth, without paying (I didn't have any change, much less the correct change), we found our way back to some civilization. By the time we did, Susie wasn't a happy camper. No more hand-holding and recitations of God's blessings. With one wrong turn (okay, maybe more than that), I had gone from feeling like Susie's Captain America to Captain Kangaroo. Our night was going downhill fast.

Any hopes of salvaging the evening were dashed when I stopped at a convenience mart under the pretense of buying gas. Actually, I was hoping to steal a glance at a map, but I wasn't about to tell Susie that. When I got out to pump the gas, Susie bolted into the store. I figured she needed to freshen up a bit after our exciting trip through the California backcountry. But when I walked into the store, Susie was engaged in a humorous and animated conversation with some tattooed hunk behind the counter. He was smiling and laughing, she was smiling and laughing, and he was giving her . . . directions!

Is there a greater blow to a man's ego? Is there a lower place on the male food chain than that reserved for the loser whose wife has to ask some California dude with bulging biceps for directions, because her husband can't drive, hold his wife's hand, and navigate at the same time? My self-esteem having been sufficiently bruised, I slunk back to the car and sulked all the way to the hotel—while following the hunk's directions. I mumbled a really weak prayer with Susie before bed and pouted my way into a terrible, listless sleep. A really great day had ended in a really bad night.

And to think, we were there to do a DVD on marriage.

Buckle Your Seat Belts

Welcome to the wonderful world of marriage. Can you think of another relationship that has the potential to take you to such relational extremes—pleasure and pain, joy and sorrow, intimacy and isolation? Marriage can be exciting, entertaining, humorous, exhilarating, inspiring, rewarding, and adventurous. It can also be really, really hard. For me, marriage is the summit point of my relational world. It is, without question, the relationship that requires the most from me and offers the greatest potential for intimacy and joy.

Culturally, the institution of marriage seems to have a perennial black eye. Maybe that's because marriage is so challenging or because so many forces seem to be vying against it. But whatever the reasons, marriage, at least in Western culture, is in real trouble.

You've probably heard the gloomy statistics—today in the United States, there are more couples living together outside of marriage,[1] and over 50 percent of all marriages end in divorce. Prenuptials and postnuptials dot the marriage landscape, as if every marriage is *supposed* to fail. Divorce court dockets are backed up for months, and infidelity, financial pressures, and irreconcilable differences claim new marriage victims every day.

Beyond that, many couples feel stuck in a marriage rut. While they may not actually get a divorce, they live relationally separate lives. They share bills, beds, and bathrooms, but little else. They raise kids together but frequently fail to model an inspiring version of marriage to which their kids can aspire. In short, not enough couples actually enjoy the intimacy, security, and love that God designed for marriage.

But marriage doesn't have to be the gloom-and-doom story that culture is trying to make it. Many married couples today, although they rarely make headlines, enjoy deep and meaningful relationships. Their marriages endure miscarriages, bankruptcies, unemployment, and even long-term illness. These marriages produce healthy, happy children, span multiple decades, end only at death, and inspire others to emulate them. Such marriages are neither farfetched nor fairy tales; rather, they're what God intends for each of us who are married, and that's precisely why we need to pray every day for our marriages.

Pray Big Prayer Starter

Ask God to give you his dream for your marriage. Pray that you and your spouse won't settle for mediocrity in your marriage.

Prayer That Gets Things Done

There is a clear biblical pattern for prayer that keeps you from wondering if you're praying correctly and helps you pray with a clear focus on God's will. It's what I call *pinpoint praying*. Through pinpoint praying, you can approach God with confidence and feel right at home making big requests of him. Pinpoint prayers speak right to the heart of God because of their two major characteristics: they're biblical and they're specific.

Biblical praying means that you use the Scriptures as your primary guide for directing and wording your prayers. I discovered years ago that my own words couldn't compete with the language, heart, and attitude expressed in the inspired words of Scripture—and they didn't need to. Rather than fumbling around in prayer, trying to figure out what to ask God and how to say it, I started letting the Bible do the talking for me.

Here's how it works: I read my Bible just about every day. As I do, I'm constantly discovering verses that say exactly what I want God to do in me, my marriage, my family, my ministry, my hometown, my nation, and so on. When I read a verse that clearly expresses my heart for something, I write a set of initials representing that person or thing next to that verse in my Bible. For example, if the verse speaks to what I want God to do in me, I write my initials in the margin. If it speaks to my wife or kids, I write theirs.

Praying the Scriptures helps me focus my heart more on what God wants and less on what I want. The inspired and

17

authoritative teachings of God's Word train me to think and pray within a biblical framework. I know my prayers carry a powerful punch before God's throne because I'm praying in the precise language God has already used to express what he wants to do. Biblical prayers are much more effective than the kinds of prayers we've all been tempted to pray, such as, *Lord, help my husband to get his sorry rear end off the couch,* or *Lord, please limit my wife to speaking only ten thousand words a day.*

Pinpoint prayers are also specific. A few years ago God convicted me about the broad, aimless nature of my prayers. I started listening to what I and others around me were asking God for. I, perhaps like you, was guilty of praying benign, sweeping prayers that never really asked anything specific of God. I would ask him to be with or to bless someone, when the Bible teaches that God was already doing both of those things. My prayers, including those for my marriage, didn't have any teeth in them. There just wasn't much substance. The Holy Spirit basically nudged me and said, *Why are you asking me to do what I'm already doing? Pray for something dramatic, something that requires faith. Pray for something big!*

Then I started pinpoint praying. Along with using the Bible as my prayer guide, I started asking very specific and focused things of God. Instead of asking God to be with my wife, I asked him to make her holy, to protect her from the pull of materialism, to heal her of specific wounds, to expand her ministry impact, to put truth in her heart and wisdom on her tongue. Instead of asking God to bless my marriage, I prayed that he would help Susie and me to love each other unconditionally, to model his love to the world, to willingly serve and yield to each other, and to know true intimacy.

Do you see the difference? I sure did. As my prayers became more specific to God, so did my answers from him.

The very pinpoint prayers I was praying turned into pinpoint answers for my marriage.

How do you pray for your marriage? Do you toss up the random *Lord, please be with us* kinds of prayers, or do you set very specific and biblical requests before God? I can tell you from experience, the more you focus and specify your requests for your marriage, the more direct answers you'll see.

Better Marriages Begin Here

In the pages that follow, I will help you mingle God's teachings on marriage with his promises on prayer. I want to raise your hopes and dreams for your marriage to a biblical level. I'll help you gain a biblical vision for what God wants your marriage to be. Then I'll show you how to base your prayers for your marriage on what God has said he's ready and willing to do. You won't have to waste time wondering if you're asking something of God for your marriage that isn't what he wants. Before you finish this book, you'll know what it means to pray big for your marriage. You'll be prepared to make more meaningful and significant requests of God, and you'll be equipped to pray powerful, pinpoint prayers for your marriage. You'll know how to pray with confidence and boldness for yourself and your spouse. God is ready to do kingdom-level things in your home. Are you ready to ask him for them?

In the coming chapters, you'll learn how to use the Bible as your guide to praying for your marriage. You'll learn why it's critical to love God more than you love your spouse and how to pray accordingly. You'll look at how to pray for a more authentic marriage, how to pray for spiritual maturity in marriage, and how to pray about your God-assigned marriage role. Men will learn how to pray very specific biblical promises for their wives, and women will learn how to pray with equal biblical focus for their husbands. In the book's final chapters, you'll learn how to pray for protection from temptations and distractions in marriage, and how to pray for the vision and mission that God has for your marriage.

Genesis 25:21 tells us, "Isaac prayed to the LORD on behalf of his wife . . . Rebekah." Isn't that a beautiful picture of a praying spouse? How would our marriages look if we spent less time complaining and moaning about them and more time praying big prayers on behalf of our spouses? Marriage doesn't have to be bad or boring; it can be your greatest blessing. The difference is prayer.

Pray Big Prayer Starter

Pray 2 Chronicles 7:16 for your marriage and home—
Holy God, choose us and anoint us as your people. Let your name always dwell with us. I pray that your eyes and your heart will always be turned toward us.

Pray Big Today

Are you ready to spice things up in your marriage? Are you ready to throw some fuel on your marriage fire? Are you tired of your marriage being Satan's punching bag? Are you hungry to discover God's mission for your marriage? Then keep reading. Together let's learn how to pray big for our marriages.

Verses to Pray for Your Marriage

- Matthew 21:22: *Father, because I believe, I ask boldly that you answer my prayer and do great and mighty things in my marriage.*

- John 14:13–14: *Holy God, I ask in the name of Jesus that you hear me and grant my pinpoint requests for my marriage.*
- Matthew 7:7–8: *Dear Lord, teach me to ask and to seek big things for my marriage through prayer.*

A Marriage Pinpoint Prayer

Precious God, I pray for my marriage. Please build your kingdom in our lives. I pray that you will give me hope and faith to know that you are going to do amazing and even miraculous things in my marriage. Teach me to pray powerful pinpoint prayers for myself and my spouse. Please change, anoint, protect, and strengthen my marriage through my prayers. I pray this in Jesus's name. Amen.

2

Big, Hairy, Audacious Prayers and Your Marriage

THIS GUY MUST have really messed up. That's what I kept thinking when I looked at the man seated next to his obviously angry wife at our church's membership class. I knew things weren't all rosy when she asked, "How do you forgive someone who has betrayed you?" She talked openly about her pain, her fears, and her inability and lack of desire to ever trust her offender again. I was a little shocked at how honest she was being in a roomful of strangers and how much anger she was venting at the one who had wounded her so gravely. Again I looked at her husband. He didn't appear at all bothered by her comments. He seemed almost immune to them. *That man really doesn't get it,* I thought. *He's out to lunch.* He was so calm and empathetic toward her, it was almost as if she wasn't talking about him. And then I realized she wasn't. She was talking about *God.*

23

This woman had been through a very difficult few years. One painful and personal hit after another had left her soul wearied and her faith in God shaken. She was hurt, tired, disappointed, and not sure she even wanted to still believe in him.

What does a believing husband or wife do when a spouse is in spiritual free fall? How does a Christian navigate the rough marital seas during a crisis of faith in his or her spouse? What would you do if tomorrow your husband or wife filed for spiritual bankruptcy?

In the case of this couple at our church, the husband did all that he could—*he prayed*. He faithfully and consistently went to God on behalf of his wounded bride. He asked for her healing and the restoration of her faith. He didn't preach; he didn't gripe; he didn't condemn. He waited and he prayed. And slowly, the spark in her eyes began to return. It didn't happen overnight, and it certainly wasn't easy, but his wife finally found peace with God. Her trust in him was eventually restored and her love for him deepened. Today this husband *and* his wife are raising godly children, have a strong marriage, and are leaders in our church.

Why Pray?

Without exception, the most effective resource for any marriage is prayer. While there are many tools and helps available for marriages these days, prayer is by far the most potent. It has the ability to work in the hearts of the two most important players in a marriage—the husband and wife—faster and more strategically than any tool you can buy or any counselor you might hire.

Below are just a few of the benefits of marriage prayer.

Prayer humbles you. If you consistently have a bad attitude about your marriage, prayer will help you change it. Holy moments spent before God in prayer help to place you and your marriage desires in proper perspective. Prayer has a great ability to reduce your ego and adjust your attitude.

Prayer guides you. God speaks through prayer. He teaches and imparts his wisdom through prayer. Prayer illuminates God's Word for you and guides you as you apply it to your marital issues and decisions. Do you want guidance in dealing with your marriage? Pray.

Prayer changes you. Any time spent alone with God will have an immediate effect on you. Prayer is one of God's primary sanctification tools. (Sanctification is the process through which God makes us holy.) When praying for your marriage, you're more likely to have a teachable spirit and be open to what God wants to do in *you*, rather than being stuck on what you want him to do in your spouse.

Prayer helps you see your spouse differently. In 2 Corinthians 5, the apostle Paul shared how Christ had changed his perspective on people: "So we have stopped evaluating others from a human point of view. At one time we thought of Christ merely from a human point of view. How differently we know him now! This means that anyone who belongs to Christ has become a new person. The old life is gone; a new life has begun!" (vv. 16–17 NLT). Paul confessed that while he used to judge others based on human standards, he had ceased doing so because his love for Jesus had given him a completely different take on people.

As you pray for your spouse, your view of them will change. You'll learn to see them through Jesus's eyes, not just your own. God will give you the ability to love your mate the way he does.

Prayer equips you. The assignments in Scripture given to Christian husbands and wives aren't easy. Husbands are called to love their wives just as Jesus loves them. Wives are called to live for their husbands as they would live for Christ

25

(see Eph. 5:22–33). Neither role comes naturally, even in the most Spirit-filled homes. That's why prayer is so critical in marriage. Your time before God in prayer will not only give you a vision of how you should function in marriage, but it will also equip you with the grace to actually do so.

Pray Big Prayer Starter

Pray 1 Samuel 12:23 for your marriage—*Lord, help me not to sin against you by ceasing to pray for my marriage.*

Lord, Is It Wrong for Me to Pray for the Ground to Open Up and Swallow My Husband?

How do we pray for our marriages? What types of things do we ask of God? How do we know what his will is? How can we know we're not just turning our selfish desires into prayers? Marriage prayer is too important to guess at. What should we be asking God to do in our marriages?

To get us started answering those questions, let's take a look at some common marriage prayers we might be tempted to pray but shouldn't.

Lord, please change them. This may be the most common and, I might add, ineffective marriage prayer of all. It's so easy to see your spouse as the problem. If he or she would just grow up, lose weight, not spend so much, get off the couch, get a life, stop griping, stop worrying, stop nagging, be more sexual, learn to hold down a job, loosen up, pay more attention to me, clean up the yard, clean out the attic, not travel so much, stop talking so much, help me with the kids, be more like _____ (you fill in the name), then things would be just fine! Right?

The least effective form of marriage praying is expressed in the attitude that everything wrong with the marriage

26

can be summed up in two words: my spouse. Prayers that repeatedly ask, "God, why did you do this to me?" never really accomplish anything. Such praying is self-centered and self-serving. Now don't get me wrong—God is interested in changing your spouse, but he's equally interested in changing you. It's not wrong for you to pray that God will do mighty things in your spouse's life, but, as we will see in the upcoming chapters, your prayers need to seek *God's* plans and desires, not yours.

Lord, get me out of here. This prayer represents the hearts of those who have had enough. They're sick and tired of the way their marriage is going, and they want out. They want a change; they want God to let them out of their marriage vows.

Considering the fact that at least 50 percent of all US marriages end in divorce, I imagine this prayer gets plenty of airtime before God. Whether or not a marriage is at the level of a biblically justifiable divorce is not the point. The point is that many Christian men and women walk around every day having given up on their marriages. They may or may not be seriously *looking* for a way out, but they're clearly *longing* for one.

The Bible offers much hope for those in such difficult marriage circumstances. The *Lord, get me out of here* request is typically not one that God is going to grant, except in extreme cases. God still takes our marriage covenants very seriously, even if we don't. His hope for your marriage is bigger and better than having it end in failure. If you're currently praying the *Lord, get me out of here* prayer for your marriage, what follows in this book will not only give you hope but also will give you a strategy for how to pray differently.

Lord, if you're not going to rescue me, then give me strength to endure. This is the prayer of those who have resigned

27

themselves to staying in a bad marriage the rest of their lives. They don't see a way out and certainly don't see things changing. They've not only given up on their marriage, they've given up on God.

Don't. Don't give up on your marriage and don't give up on God. To do so is to indict him of caring about other marriages but not yours. It implies that he doesn't really have the power to change you and/or your mate and give you the kind of marriage that he intended from the beginning. If you're a Christ-follower, you have countless biblical reasons to believe that God can and will still work in your marriage. To halfheartedly pray that you'll endure what he has assigned you is to aim too low, to pray too small. Jesus didn't die on the cross for you to be stuck in the rut of *Lord, help me to put up with this until I get to heaven* kind of praying. Such praying is not only a waste of time, it insults God.

It's time for you to start praying with the kind of divine intensity and gusto that Jesus died to give you. It's time for you to learn to make big asks of God for your marriage.

Big, Hairy, Audacious Prayers

Growing up, I had a mentor who used to always tell young Christian women who were looking for a husband to not settle for a hot dog when God had promised them a T-bone steak. Translation: don't marry a spiritual dud when God wants you to have a mighty man.

I believe that many of us settle for mediocrity when it comes to the level of intimacy and joy we experience in our marriages, and it's due in part to the fact that we don't ask big things of God.

In my book *Pray Big*,[1] I introduced the concept of BHAPs: Big, Hairy, Audacious Prayers. (I credit Jim Collins's discussion of Big, Hairy, Audacious Goals, or BHAGs, in his book *Built to Last* as the initial source for this concept.) A big, hairy, audacious prayer is a request that requires a miraculous response from God. It's neither presumptuous nor self-serving, and as a pinpoint prayer it is both biblical and specific. It's the kind of praying that takes quite seriously verses such as the following:

- Matthew 21:22: "If you believe, you will receive whatever you ask for in prayer."
- John 14:13–14: "And I will do whatever you ask in my name, so that the Son may bring glory to the Father. You may ask me for anything in my name, and I will do it."
- Matthew 7:7–8: "Ask and it will be given to you; seek and you will find; knock and the door will be opened to you. For everyone who asks receives; he who seeks finds; and to him who knocks, the door will be opened."

I could list multiple others. These teachings of Jesus aren't in the Bible as page fillers. He gave them to us because he wants and expects us to pray with the kind of hope and faith that they describe.

When you're praying for your marriage, don't be timid about what you ask of God. Jesus commanded us to seek and find through prayer. If we didn't need God's miraculous power for every aspect of our Christian lives, including our marriages, he wouldn't have repeatedly urged us to ask for it in prayer. So pray big! Read the Scriptures, discover God's promises, and start praying some big, hairy, audacious prayers for your marriage today.

Are you married to an unbeliever? Pray that he or she will embrace Christ and become an obedient follower. Is your marriage tense because of financial stress? Pray for

God to make you both good stewards, to equip you to get out of debt, and to help you become a generous, giving couple. Do you lack emotional intimacy? Pray for God to blow away the barriers and to grant you oneness of heart. Are you at odds with an ex-spouse or a difficult set of in-laws? Pray for healing and maturity in that relationship. In other words, don't pray to just get by; pray to prevail. Pray big!

What do you want God to do in your marriage? When you read the Bible, what stories or verses describe what you long to be true for you and your spouse? Start praying them. Ask others to pray them with you. Wherever possible and appropriate, pray them *with* your spouse. Ask God for some big, hairy, audacious dreams and promises for your marriage, and then start praying them. It might be ten days or ten years, but you will see God work in ways beyond what you could ever ask or think (see Eph. 3:20).

Pray Big Prayer Starter

Pray Philippians 4:19 for your marriage—*Lord God, please meet all the needs of our marriage according-ing to the riches of your glory that is in Jesus Christ.*

The Ultimate Divorce Buster

Did you know that Christian marriages are just as likely to end in divorce as those of non-Christians? That's right. The tragic truth is that the 50 percent divorce rate for all US marriages is the same whether the couple claims the Christian faith or not.[2] However, there are some Christian couples who experience dramatically lower divorce rates than their cultural counterparts. That group consists of couples who pray together regularly.

What do you think the divorce rate is for praying couples? Half the national average (25 percent)? One-third the national average (17 percent)? Those would certainly be better numbers. But they're still too high. Try 1 percent or less! That's right; couples who pray together have a greater than 99 percent chance of having a marriage that lasts.[3]

Are you convinced yet? Are you ready to start interceding for and with your spouse? Are you ready to begin asking God to do miraculous things in your home? Jesus died to give you the right and authority to ask for kingdom-level favor for your marriage. Don't waste his power. Start praying today!

Pray Big Today

If you're new to the adventure of prayer, here are a few suggestions to help you establish good prayer habits:

- Pray every day. It doesn't have to be long or necessarily intense, but try to have a time of prayer every day. Prayer is the spiritual equivalent of plugging your soul into a battery charger. You need it regularly. So make prayer one of your regular daily disciplines, even if it's just for a few minutes.
- Have a regular time. Try to carve out the same time of day to pray. Those of you with uncertain schedules or unpredictable circumstances may find this difficult, but give it your best shot. Making a regular time for prayer increases the chances of you actually stopping to meet with God.
- Have a regular place. When it comes to prayer, familiarity breeds consistency. New or ever-changing surroundings can be a distraction in prayer. Find a no-frills

31

place where you can meet with God without distractions. Get away from the TV, the phone, the computer, the refrigerator, your to-do list, or anything else that might compete for your attention.

- Have a regular system. Earlier I mentioned how I use my Bible in prayer. I have a systematic plan for reading the Word, and I let my daily readings drive what I pray for. I also have lists of names in my Bible that I bring before God every day. Having a plan reduces the time you spend warming up to prayer. It helps you to jump right into praying and not waste time wondering what you should pray for.

One Big, Hairy, Audacious Prayer for Your Marriage

The rest of this book is dedicated to helping you identify biblical and specific requests you can take to God daily for your marriage. When you're finished, you'll have a whole list of BHAPs you can begin asking God for. But before we move on, I'd like to suggest one very powerful pinpoint prayer you can start praying today for your marriage: *Lord, please give us the kind of marriage that Jesus made available to us through his death.*

In John 10:10, Jesus set a high bar for the kind of life he wants his followers to know: "I came that they may have life, and have it abundantly" (NASB). The abundant life that Jesus spoke of is inseparably linked to his coming to earth and dying. He wasn't just speaking of life in heaven; he meant for us to enjoy a full and blessing-rich life right now, today.

Abundant life doesn't mean that you're free from pain or that you suddenly become financially well-off. It means that you know and enjoy Christ's presence, power, and peace in your life, regardless of your circumstances.

Start praying that for your marriage. Pray that God will give you a full and abundant marriage relationship. Ask God to grant you all the favor, anointing, and provision that Jesus made available to you through his death. Pray that your marriage will know Jesus's presence, power, and peace. That's a biblical and specific pinpoint prayer that God will answer.

Verses to Pray for Your Marriage

- 2 Corinthians 5:16: *Lord, please help me to see my spouse through your eyes. Help me to love and to have compassion for my spouse the way you do.*
- John 10:10: *Father, protect us from the thief who comes to kill, steal, and destroy our marriage. Give us the abundant life that Jesus promised.*
- Jeremiah 31:3: *Lord, help our marriage to mirror your everlasting love and loving-kindness.*

A Marriage Pinpoint Prayer

Holy Father, I love you and praise your holy name. You are my mighty God. I pray that you will build your kingdom in my marriage. Please grant my spouse and me the abundant life that Jesus gave us through his death. Please expose and remove any barriers or relationships in our lives that keep us from knowing all the joy you intend for our marriage. Grant us the favor, peace, blessing, protection, power, and presence of Jesus in our marriage. Amen.

3

PRAYING FOR
SECOND PLACE

SUSIE AND I got engaged at a romantic restaurant in
the tiny hamlet of Glen Haven, Colorado. It was the
summer of 1984. I was 22; she was 20.

I'd chosen the site of my "great proposal" very carefully.
The Glen Haven Inn is surrounded by a raging mountain
river, gorgeous pines, and towering Rockies. The table I chose
was strategically placed under a beautiful stained-glass window. It portrayed a sword-wielding, handsome young knight
rescuing a lovely damsel from a vicious dragon—an image
that seemed appropriate for Susie and me.

Susie and I had been ring hunting and talking about marriage for a couple of years. I'd asked her father and mine for
permission to be married. She knew the "great proposal"
was coming; she just didn't know when.

If you're wondering why I keep referring to the event as
the "great proposal," it's because that is exactly how I viewed

it. Proposing to the woman of my dreams was a major event for me. I'd seen enough episodes of *The Newlywed Game* to know that brides have very long memories when it comes to bad, unromantic, or botched marriage proposals. I had no intentions of making such a blunder. Add to that the facts that Susie and I had dated on and off for nearly six years, that the last time we broke up was three months before we got engaged, and that Susie had taken my best friend to her senior prom, and you get the sense that our finally getting engaged was nothing short of an act of God. Yep, this was a big night for both of us. I had to get it right.

But when I nearly severed my Adam's apple while shaving just an hour before our big date, I knew things might not go as planned. I cut myself so badly that the result could have easily passed for a tracheotomy. I greeted Susie that night with a giant, gaping hole in my neck. I looked like a Cyclops, but with a third oozing eye growing where my Adam's apple used to be. It wasn't a pretty sight. I wasn't yet a candidate for the "Dud Groom" award on *The Newlywed Game*, but I had taken a step closer. Oh well, I still had hopes for our romantic dinner. Maybe the candlelit setting of the Glen Haven Inn, along with my humble proposal and ring unveiling, could salvage the night.

Dinner went really well, right up until the moment I wanted to actually ask Susie to marry me. While she went to the restroom after dinner, I set the ring on the ledge below the stained-glass window. When she returned, I intended to grab the ring off the ledge, fall to my knees, and ask for her lovely hand in marriage. In my excitement, however, I actually knocked the ring off the ledge onto the wooden floor below.

It's amazing how a woman can instinctively recognize the sound of a diamond ring bouncing along a wooden floor. Susie instantly perked up and asked cheerfully, "What was that?" while I fumbled around under the table, trying to find the ring. When I finally rose up and handed it to her, my face was red, my neck orifice was oozing from the gravitational effects of my head being inverted under the table, and all I could muster was a weak, "Will you please marry me?" Susie graciously acquiesced. Meanwhile, I could hear a phone ringing in the background. It was Bob Eubanks, calling to book me for *The Newlywed Game*.

A Marriage Proposal for the Ages

Against the backdrop of my rather disastrous attempt at a "great proposal," I'd like to tell you about the greatest marriage proposal of all time. But it's not what you think. This proposal wasn't from a prospective groom to his bride—at least not in the traditional sense—and it wasn't birthed in human romance or emotion. The greatest marriage proposal was from the Lord Jesus to each of us. Jesus has invited every living soul into a relationship with him that's more meaningful and beautiful than any earthly marriage. Listen to his invitation: "Come to me, all you who are weary and burdened, and I will give you rest. Take my yoke upon you and learn from me, for I am gentle and humble in heart, and you will find rest for your souls. For my yoke is easy and my burden is light" (Matt. 11:28–30).

Aren't those some incredible words from Jesus? Did you hear what he offered? Relationship—"come to me." Spiritual provision—"I will give you rest." Partnership—"take my yoke upon you." Insight—"learn from me." Comfort—"I am gentle and humble in heart." Relief—"my yoke is easy and my burden is light." Did you ever hear a more profound or appealing proposal? That's what it is—a marriage proposal. Jesus invites each of us—male and female—to "marry" ourselves to him first and foremost. He invites us into a spiritual union with him that requires our purest love and instantly becomes our most important relationship. Jesus taught that all other relationships, including marriage, must come after our relationship with him. If we ever get those priorities out of order, then every relationship we have will suffer.

Now, you may be thinking, *Wait a minute. How can I love someone else, even Jesus, more than my spouse? Isn't my marriage supposed to be the most important relationship I have?* The answer is *no.* Your marriage relationship is your *second* most important relationship. Everything God wants you to be in marriage you'll learn from your relationship with Christ. He has to be first. It's his rightful place as Lord. You don't want your husband or wife to love you more than anything else. You want him or her to love Jesus more than anything or anyone else, including you. Only the person who is first "married" to Jesus can properly and adequately fulfill his or her biblical role in marriage.

Pray Big Prayer Starter

Pray that you will love Jesus more than any other person in your life. Pray the same for your spouse. Pray that your respective relationships with Jesus will be your highest priority.

Have you accepted Jesus's marriage invitation? Has your spouse? Let's look at Scripture and see what happens when Jesus isn't first in our lives.

~~Three~~ Six Strikes and You're Still Not Out

The sun was high in the sky as Jesus considered the woman before him. She had come to draw water at the historic site of Jacob's well just outside the small village of Sychar. It was the middle of the day. Most women came to the well in early morning or late evening to avoid carrying their heavy water jugs in the heat of the day. This woman had come at an inconvenient time, perhaps to avoid the crowds—including their judgmental stares and gossipy tongues—that she would no doubt encounter at a more convenient hour. She wasn't a full-fledged prostitute, but to her neighbors, she might as well have been. So this woman of the night came to draw water in the middle of the day.

Jesus engaged her in conversation. It would have been easy enough, even expected, for him to ignore her. In that culture, men and women who were strangers didn't speak. Besides that, Jews and Samaritans, who were bitter religious rivals, never interacted socially. For Jesus to address this woman was surprising to say the least. But Jesus knew what he was doing. The woman's wounded soul needed what he alone could offer. Jesus decided to approach her through a topic she could relate to—thirst.

> **Jesus:** I'm thirsty. Will you please draw some water for me?
>
> **Woman:** Why are you speaking to me? You know Jews don't deal with Samaritans, especially Samaritan women.
>
> **Jesus:** If you knew who I was and what I could offer, *you* would be asking *me* for water. Then I would give you living water.
>
> **Woman:** Excuse me, sir, but you look a little unprepared to be talking about giving away water. You're empty-handed. How do you intend to draw out this living water you speak of? Who do you think you are, sir?
>
> **Jesus:** I'm not talking about *this* water from *this* well. I'm talking about the kind of water that I alone can offer. If you drink it, you'll never thirst again. In fact, the

water I give you will produce a spring of eternal life within you.

Woman (not getting it): Sounds good to me. I'd love to never be thirsty again and not have to keep coming back to this well and refilling these jugs. Give me this water!

Jesus (cutting to the chase): Go get your husband.

Woman (after a long pause, her eyes looking downward): I'm not married.

Jesus: Close enough. You've been married five times. The man you share a bed with now isn't your husband. So I guess you're right when you tell me you're "not married."

Woman (after another long pause): Let me guess—you're a prophet. Right?

(For a more literal and inspired version of this conversation, see John 4:5–19.)

Do you see what Jesus did in that conversation? He engaged the woman about a symptom (her thirst) but then moved quickly to the source of her problem (her sin). The woman had made the terrible and all-too-common mistake of looking to other humans to meet needs that only God can meet. If marriage can satisfy a soul, then this woman should have been in spiritual nirvana. As it was, she was in a spiritual wasteland. Her five marriages had been unable to fill the needs of her starving and wounded soul. When Jesus found her, she'd given up on marriage but not on her search. Tragically, she was still looking in the wrong place.

Pray Big Prayer Starter

Ask God to pour out his living water on your marriage. Pray that you and your spouse will thirst more for God and his living water than for each other.

Broken Wells and Dusty Lips

The mistake made by the woman described in John 4 is one many people still make today. Somehow they believe that the right marriage recipe can yield the ultimate happy life. They're wrong, and that's why so many relationships end up failing. If people go into a marriage hoping that a relationship with another human can somehow complete them, they're going to be very disappointed. As humans—sinful, broken, and inconsistent—we can't meet the longings of our own souls, much less someone else's.

Trying to draw spiritual life from another spiritually depraved human is a poor relational strategy. But we do it all the time. People enter into relationships, move in together, become sexually active, and even marry in hopes of finding ultimate fulfillment. But that just doesn't work. Such relationships are nothing more than one desperate and needy person trying to suck life from another. It's what a friend of mine used to refer to as "two ticks, no dog."

The Bible offers a more sobering description of the same phenomena. The prophet Jeremiah called it idolatry. Listen to his words, spoken to the soon-to-be exiled nation of Judah nearly seven hundred years before Christ: " 'Has a nation ever changed its gods? (Yet they are not gods at all.) But my people have exchanged their Glory for worthless idols. Be appalled at this, O heavens, and shudder with great horror,' declares the LORD. 'My people have committed two sins: They have forsaken me, the spring of living water, and have dug their own cisterns, broken cisterns that cannot hold water'" (Jer. 2:11–13).

In these challenging words to Judah's priests and leaders, Jeremiah accuses them of making two very foolish decisions. First, they abandoned their faith and dependence on God. Second, they put their confidence in dead, lifeless

41

idols that could neither hear their prayers nor provide for their needs.

Now, before we judge these folks too harshly, we have to acknowledge that we do the exact same thing. While swearing allegiance to God with our mouths, we look to things (idols) for ultimate fulfillment. You can name them—money, power, job security, talents, sex, popularity, possessions, and even relationships. Our idols are much more glamorous and sophisticated than the gold statues worshiped by Jeremiah's contemporaries, but they're idols nonetheless. And they're equally insufficient at meeting the needs of the human soul.

For those of us who are married, a likely and tempting object of our misplaced loyalties is our spouse. Men and women make rotten gods, but we still deify them. It's not that we really see them as divine, because we know they're not. But it's easy to slip into the rut of looking to the person we love most in the world to meet the deepest and most pressing needs of our soul. We lean heavily on them, somehow thinking that their approval, their love, their smile, their affection, their words, their presence, or their blessing will ultimately give us life. I can't tell you the number of times I've counseled Christian women who were dating or married to complete spiritual duds simply because they couldn't face *not* having a man in their life. The social stigma and personal blow of feeling unwanted and unattractive was more than they could handle. They settled for any guy they could get in the misguided hope that being *wanted* would make them whole.

The same misplaced loyalties can even creep into healthy Christian marriages. Many committed Christ-followers are equally guilty of paying verbal homage to God but looking to their spouse for their security and self-esteem. It's easy to do. I speak from experience.

Looking for Love in All the Wrong Places

I told you earlier about my failed attempt at the "great proposal." Well, I'm embarrassed to admit that I was equally unsuccessful at the "great illusion." The "great illusion," as I call it, was my attempt to look and act put-together and in control while I was actually insecure and emotionally needy. I was a Christian and a pastor, and yet I was guilty of off-the-charts levels of idolatry. The object of my worship and idolatry? My wife, Susie.

My idolatry wasn't overt or deliberate, but it was real. While proclaiming Christ to others and teaching them how to let Jesus meet their needs, I was actually more dependent on my own wife than my Lord. I looked to Susie for my self-esteem and my security. If Susie and I were in a good place relationally, I was okay. If Susie was angry at me or disappointed in me, my self-esteem and security plummeted. If she was distant or just needing some space, I took it personally. I may have been paying tribute to Jesus with my mouth, but the person who clearly had the most control over me was Susie. It was a position she did not want, but I gave it to her nonetheless. Doing so totally devastated my relationship with God, and it also created significant pressure for Susie. Not only was she responsible for her own spiritual condition, she was also unwittingly responsible for mine. She had to care for and lead two souls, not one. Susie couldn't afford to have a bad day, to not be "in the mood," or to just want some downtime. The wrong response from her could throw me into a total spiritual tailspin.

Tragically, I was a living example of Jeremiah's graphic prophecy. I had forsaken my glory, the fountain of living water, and had dug dry and empty wells for myself. I was trying to draw life from a source (Susie) that was neither equipped nor able to provide it. And it was killing both of us.

So what happened? How did I break out of my self-imposed idolatry? After a series of God-directed events and conversations, Susie and I came to the conclusion that I needed significant emotional healing. Susie started praying for me. I remember when she first told me that she was praying for God to heal me. I hadn't really thought that I needed healing. I was wrong.

Susie had enough sense to know that what we were experiencing was neither normal nor healthy. She also had the maturity to know that she couldn't change me. So she prayed. Over the next decade, God broke through my proud exterior and shattered my heart. He showed me what grace really was, exposed the idols in my life, and set me free from years of sin and misplaced loyalties. I'm probably not overstating things when I say that Susie's prayers and God's gracious answers to them saved our marriage.

What about you? Can you relate? Are you in a marriage that can be described more by broken wells than by streams of living water? Are you too dependent on your spouse? Is he or she too dependent on you? Do either of you crater emotionally in the face of marital conflict? Are you too reliant upon sexual intimacy for your self-esteem? Do you feel trapped in the other's codependence? If so, then start praying! God wants to heal you, your spouse, and your marriage.

Pray Big Prayer Starter

Ask God to help you and your mate have your highest emotional and spiritual needs met by Jesus.

When It's Good to Finish Second

In the book of Revelation, Jesus rebuked the Christ-followers in Ephesus for having their priorities out of line: "Yet I hold this against you: You have forsaken your first love" (Rev. 2:4). The first love whom they had forsaken was Jesus himself. As King of Kings and Lord of Lords, he doesn't fit well in second place. Colossians 1:18 says that it is natural for Jesus to be first in everything. That includes your relationships.

When you pray for your marriage, pray that you and your spouse will be comfortable in second place. It's not a bad thing to come behind Jesus. That's exactly what God wants for us in marriage—Jesus first, spouse second.

Couples who overcome the temptation to put each other over Jesus will know increased intimacy and relational security. They'll feel less pressure to perform a certain way in marriage, and they'll be free to love the way God created them to. The "Jesus first, spouse second" mind-set will create a flow of spiritual momentum and favor from the Holy Spirit that will permeate every area of the marriage relationship.

Pray Big Today

As you learn to look to Jesus for spiritual vitality in marriage, you'll begin to see many areas of your relationship changed by your new perspective. Here are some ways you can pray for your marriage to be strengthened as you and your spouse love Jesus first:

- Pray that conflict won't cause either of you to shut down or retreat emotionally. Ask God to make you secure enough in him to not feel threatened and unstable when you and your spouse disagree.
- Pray that you'll learn the disciplines involved in drinking from the living waters of the Holy Spirit. Ask God to teach you how to enjoy his presence and to be filled by his Spirit.

- Pray that you will always have the right motives when dealing with your spouse. Ask God to give you a servant's heart toward him or her. Pray that you will always approach your mate with the intention to give, not take.
- Pray for a healthy and biblical perspective on sex. Ask God to help you see the act of sex as a renewal of your marriage covenant and as an opportunity to graciously show your love and commitment to your spouse.
- Ask that you'll never make an idol of your spouse or of trying to have a "perfect" marriage. Pray that you will always prioritize your love for Jesus and that you will never let anything come between your heart and his.

Verses about Loving Jesus to Pray for Your Marriage

- Revelation 2:4–5: *Father, you are my first love. Help me to always love you and worship you first. I pray that my wife will love you more than she loves me. Help us to never stray from following you.*
- Exodus 20:3–4: *Lord God, you command us to never worship any gods but you, the one true God. Help me and my husband to love and worship you alone. Help us to always keep you first in our lives and to never place anything or anyone above you.*
- John 7:37–38: *Jesus, you promised that if we're thirsty, we can come to you and drink. Show us how to drink from your spring of living waters. Help us to never settle for the dry and dusty wells the world offers. Help my spouse and me to never try to "drink" from each other, and please forgive us for the times that we have. Help us to look only to you as the source of our spiritual lives.*

A Marriage Pinpoint Prayer

Holy Father, I pray for my marriage. I thank you for giving me a loving wife. I pray that she will fall passionately in love with you. I pray that she will look to you for her strength, her hope, her joy, her self-esteem, and her security. I pray that she will know the sweetness of loving Jesus. Be her first love, O God. Create a holy fire in my wife for you. I pray this for me as well. Help us to love you more than we love each other. I pray this in Jesus's awesome name. Amen.

4

PRAYING FOR
EMOTIONAL INTIMACY

I T WAS THE week after Labor Day in 2006. My two daughters and I were up late one night watching Family Channel reruns when we stumbled upon the memorial service for Steve Irwin, the famous Crocodile Hunter. The service was being broadcast live from Australia, and it immediately enthralled us.

The broadcast included brief comments by several celebrities who had known Irwin. One was actor Kevin Costner. Costner commented that Irwin was the most authentic person he had ever known. He said there was absolutely no pretense with the man. Steve Irwin, according to Costner, was totally the real deal.

Those comments struck me. Not because I doubted what he said. I believe that the passionate Irwin was completely authentic. What struck me was that Costner stated that he had never known a more authentic human being. Maybe

49

Costner was overstating his case, or maybe he wasn't think-ing about his immediate family. But his comments did raise a good question: how far into your relational world do you have to go to find a truly authentic person? Is that person a rela-tive, a co-worker, a member of your small group or Sunday school class? True authenticity is a difficult trait to find in people today. Maybe that's why people like Steve Irwin stick out in our minds. Authentic relationships—relationships in which both parties are equally real and are extremely close because of it—are even harder to find.

It doesn't have to be that way. God designed marriage to be the one human relationship that guarantees authenticity and the intimacy it produces. You shouldn't have to look any farther than your own marriage to find your most intimate and meaningful relationship. In this chapter, we're going to learn how to pray for true emotional intimacy. In other words, we'll see what it means to pray that you and your spouse will be *naked without shame*.

Naked (Adjective): Bare, Nude, Defenseless, Uncovered

To fully understand what God has in mind for our marital intimacy, and to be better equipped to pray biblically for it, we need to go back to God's initial words on the matter. In the second chapter of the Bible, in the setting of original creation, God tells us how he feels about marital intimacy: "For this reason a man will leave his father and mother and be united to his wife, and they will become one flesh. The man and his wife were both naked, and they felt no shame" (Gen. 2:24–25).

Several interesting ideas can be found in these profound words, which we need to keep in mind when praying for our marriages. First, God described the union between a man and a woman as "one flesh." It's difficult to overemphasize the significance of this idea. Remember that the event leading to the creation of Eve was Adam's survey of the animal kingdom without finding a suitable partner: "Now the LORD God had formed out of the ground all the beasts of the field and all the birds of the air. He brought them to the man to see what he would name them; and whatever the man called each living creature, that was its name. So the man gave names to all the livestock, the birds of the air and all the beasts of the field. But for Adam no suitable helper was found" (Gen. 2:19–20).

Aren't you glad that Adam didn't find a suitable mate? I think Adam showed great levels of insight and discernment there. What if, while God was parading the animals before him, Adam had suddenly said, "Hold on, God. Stop right there. Helloooo, kangaroo!" I'm really glad that didn't happen.

God wanted Adam to see just how special Eve was going to be. He wanted Adam to know that what he needed was a special creation of God, someone with whom he could be completely one. His phrase "one flesh" is the highest compliment God could pay a human relationship. It's also the high standard he set for our marriage commitment. God wants and expects us to experience in marriage a level of unity unmatched by any other relationship we have. He wants us to be *one*.

Another interesting idea is that, as we saw in the last chapter, God established marriage as our number one priority *after* our relationship with him. He instructed all men and women who choose to marry to leave their family of origin and create a new family unit. That new family is to be their relational priority and merit their best efforts. It's like God is saying, "If you're going to be married, then I expect you to throw yourself fully into the relationship. I want you and your spouse to cling to each other more than to anyone else." When that type of no-holds-barred commitment is manifested in marriage, it will help build serious marital intimacy.

Finally, God expects us to be fully exposed to and vulnerable with each other in our marriage relationship. The phrase "the man and his wife were both naked, and they felt no shame" is both descriptive and poignant. It's obvious that Moses, the author of Genesis, was referencing, at the least, Adam and Eve's physical nakedness. He was describing the time before sin entered the picture and shattered the union that Adam and Eve had with God and with each other. After their rebellion, God clothed them with animal skins. They were no longer innocent, and thus their physical nakedness was no longer appropriate.

But Moses's words refer to much more than just Adam and Eve's initial lack of clothing. Implied in the Hebrew phrase are the ideas of vulnerability, authenticity, and safety. Neither Adam nor Eve felt any need to hide from the other. They had no secrets, and they certainly had no fear of feeling shame or rejection. They were completely exposed to each other—physically, emotionally, and mentally—without any fear of a negative reaction from the other. It was the safest, purest relationship in the world, and it represents exactly what God wants you to know in marriage. Such intimacy is impossible to achieve without you and your spouse both having meaningful, thriving relationships with God.

Pray Big Prayer Starter

Pray that your marriage will be relationally safe.
Ask God to enable you to cultivate emotional
openness and honesty in your marriage.
Pray that you and your spouse will trust
each other more than anyone else.

Shirt, Shoes, and Pants Required

As I type these words, I'm sitting at a McDonald's in the Denver airport on my way home from a midwinter study break. The airport is very crowded, and I'm surrounded by people from all over the world. As I look around, I notice something about every one of them that we usually take for granted: there's not a naked person in sight.

Nakedness isn't in our nature. Even though we're born naked, we quickly learn to cover ourselves and to stay that way. But as I look again at the crowd around me, I see something else. I see men and women who are equally clothed—protected—emotionally. Almost as quickly as we learn to cover ourselves physically, we also learn to cover up emotionally. Conventional wisdom tells us that the world is a rough-and-tumble place. If we're going to survive, we had better guard our hearts. And so we learn to protect our innermost feelings—our fears, our hopes, our hurts, our needs—even in marriage. Few of us do relational authenticity well. Most of us just fake it.

How good are you at being real and authentic? It doesn't take much to make us shut down our hearts and take a vow of emotional celibacy. Has something caused you to build a wall around your heart? Did your parents divorce, or did you lose a parent when you were young? Were you the victim of emotional, verbal, or physical abuse? Did you have few healthy friendships or too many failed dating relationships growing up? Were you overweight, not very athletic or pretty, or an underachiever? Did you experience the ridicule that often goes with not hitting the cultural high bar for what makes you "acceptable"?

Any of these situations can have a major negative impact on your emotional health and your willingness to be vulnerable. If you go into marriage without the healing of God's

Holy Spirit in these areas, you can bet that being naked without shame isn't going to happen easily. But these types of issues don't have to be relational deal breakers.

Pray Big Prayer Starter

Start praying today for your own emotional healing. Pray for your spouse's. Ask God to heal the wounds that may have damaged your ability to be emotionally authentic.

The Benefits of Being Naked

If we're going to pray diligently and passionately for our marriage intimacy, we need to have a good grasp of the payoffs and benefits of relational authenticity. Let's spend a moment reminding ourselves of why God placed such value on nakedness in marriage.

* *Authenticity opens the door to intimacy.* If intimacy is being fully exposed to (naked with) another person, then authenticity is taking off your clothes. Being authentic and real with your spouse is the first step to experiencing intimacy with him or her. Many marriages exist only on superficial emotional levels because neither spouse is willing to take the risk of being real. Remember, the road to intimacy is paved with authenticity. So get real.

* *Authenticity yields comfort.* In Matthew 5:4, Jesus taught that only those who mourn will be comforted. As uninviting as mourning may sound, it's actually a vital part of authenticity. The acts of mourning, or grieving, to which Jesus referred include verbal and even physical expressions of inner, emotional realities—perhaps grief over sin, a failed friendship, a career disappointment,

54

or hurtful words spoken by another. But simply put, mourning is an outward demonstration of your inner condition. Mourning helps you vent your pain and alerts your spouse to your need to work through the healing process in a certain area. Those who choose to be real will receive the comfort they need. But those who hide their true feelings and are inauthentic won't be comforted.

• *Authenticity allows you to experience God's love.* There is obviously some risk involved in baring your soul to another person, but God designed marriage to be the perfect safe place for such risk taking. In marriage, we're supposed to be able to share our deepest fears, dreams, and hopes without the risk of rejection. When your spouse responds lovingly to your confession of sin, or when you respond in grace to his or her emotional pain, you both have the chance to model God's love to each other. Authenticity is a great avenue through which God's love can flow, because it gives you and your mate the chance to respond to each other as God would respond to you.

• *Authenticity removes any need for pretense.* Once, when I was leading a Bible study on authenticity, I asked the group what the advantages of truth-telling were. I was looking for answers like those I've listed: increased intimacy, the chance to be fully loved—spiritual things like that. A crusty, sixty-something man raised his hand and then answered in a slow drawl, "You know, the advantage to telling the truth is that you never have to remember what you said." It took me a moment to understand what the guy was saying. But then I realized that he was on to something. Authentic people don't have to lie. They don't have to fake it. Authentic husbands and wives never have to pretend with each other, and they certainly don't have to keep up with their stories. They just live in the truth and let the chips fall where they may.

- *Authenticity enables you to be fully known.* The tragic reality is that many Christ-followers live through decades of marriage without ever being fully known by their spouse. They fear that if they get too honest about who they really are, their spouse will judge them, think less of them, pull away from them, or, worst of all, reject them. Many Christians don't think they can afford to be relationally real. They assume that their spouse can't handle their full disclosure, and, sadly, they never give them the opportunity to.

  But frequently they're wrong. The very spouse who you think will reject you may actually love you more and be drawn closer to you through your honesty with him or her. How can you be fully loved and accepted in marriage (which is God's design) if you don't give your mate the opportunity to fully love and accept you? Authenticity opens the door for you and your spouse to really know everything about each other. But such a level of openness is a choice. Only those couples who take the risk of true relational authenticity will discover the buried treasure of marital intimacy.

Authentic living can also produce a little short-term chaos. Relational vulnerability doesn't always draw immediate applause from others. It may be met with some initial shock, hurt, surprise, or even anger. But in the long term, it frees both you and your spouse to live in the light before God and with each other.

Consider these authentic statements that individuals make every day in marriage. While they might bring short-term tension to a relationship, they will yield long-term freedom.

- When you talk that way, you really hurt me.
- When we got married, I wasn't a virgin.
- On my last out-of-town trip, I watched a pornographic movie in the hotel room.
- I said some things about you to my small group that I probably shouldn't have.
- I was abused as a child.
- I think I'm an alcoholic.
- I feel a deep sense of fear and insecurity.
- I'm afraid I'm going to lose my job.
- I think I have some abiding anger toward you.
- I'm not sure I'm really a Christian.
- I have an eating disorder.
- I am terrified of death.
- I've been spending money and hiding it from you.
- I think God is calling me to the ministry.
- I need to confess something to you.
- I don't feel like you ever really listen to me.
- I wish we could spend more time together.
- I am really struggling in my relationship with God.
- There's a person at the office I'm starting to feel attracted to.
- I'm afraid your drinking is hurting our relationship.

Jesus taught us that truth sets us free (see John 8:32). As difficult as some of these authentic confessions may be to make initially, couples who practice such levels of relational nakedness also experience levels of intimacy and oneness that can't be reached otherwise. They truly are free to love each other without pretense.

Pray Big Prayer Starter

Pray that God will help you and your mate to have a meaningful, revealing, and intimate conversation in the next two weeks.

The Secret to Authenticity

Let's consider Genesis 2:25 again: "The man and his wife were both naked, and they felt no shame." Have you ever wondered how that was possible? How were Adam and Eve able to be so authentic and not fear rejection? Why was nakedness so easy for them?

Remember that Adam and Eve lived in a sinless environment. There were no barriers of sin to inhibit their relationship with God. They were able to be authentic and naked with each other without fear because they were totally safe in their respective spiritual relationships. Adam and Eve both experienced higher levels of intimacy in their relationship with God than they had with each other. As a result, authenticity in their human relationship came naturally for them.

But what happened when they sinned? They immediately realized they were naked—exposed and unprotected—and they covered themselves. Isn't that tragic? The fall of Adam and Eve and their subsequent retreat to their separate corners is a graphic example of what happens in our marriages when our hearts aren't right with God. If we're not being fully authentic and open with God, there's no way we can be naked with each other. That's why true marital intimacy requires that we be right with God. That's why marital intimacy requires prayer.

The Ultimate Example of Nakedness

When praying for marital authenticity, pray for the kind of heart and authentic spirit that Jesus modeled for us. He is the best example of true authentic living.

Consider the night before Jesus's crucifixion. In a display of complete humility and brokenness his disciples had not seen before, Jesus asked Peter, James, and John to support him in his precrucifixion agony. Matthew gives us a vivid description of the scene: "He took Peter and the two sons of Zebedee along with him, and he began to be sorrowful and troubled. Then he said to them, 'My soul is overwhelmed with sorrow to the point of death. Stay here and keep watch with me'" (Matt. 26:37–38). Jesus made no effort to appear strong or to act the part of the fearless leader for his disciples. His heart was breaking, and he wanted his followers to know it.

In another classic scene of humility and vulnerability (also from the night before his death), Jesus washed his disciples' feet. John, an eyewitness, recalled the incident: "Jesus knew that the Father had put all things under his power, and that he had come from God and was returning to God; so he got up from the meal, took off his outer clothing, and wrapped a towel around his waist. After that, he poured water into a basin and began to wash his disciples' feet, drying them with the towel that was wrapped around him" (John 13:3–5).

Did you notice what John said about Jesus? "Jesus knew that the Father had put all things under his power, and that he had come from God and was returning to God" (v. 3).

59

Jesus was completely secure in his relationship with God. His status before God was not in question. He could take the risk of being emotionally vulnerable with his disciples because he was firmly locked into the relationship that mattered most—the one with his Father. Jesus humbled himself by washing the disciples' feet (a role typically reserved for slaves), and he even shared his deepest fears and pains with them. That's the kind of authenticity we want to exhibit in our marriages. That's the type of courage we want to have with our spouses. And that's the level of vulnerability we need to pray for.

Now apply this concept specifically to your marriage. The ability to be naked without shame in marriage isn't dependent primarily upon your mutual acceptance of each other, although that's certainly a part of the equation. The first step toward relational intimacy is knowing you are secure in your relationship with God. If you want to find the "one flesh" level of intimacy that God designed for marriage, then you must first secure your heart in your heavenly Father's love. Read his Word. Pray daily. Worship openly and passionately. Love him first and foremost. Only then will you be free enough to love and accept your spouse unconditionally. Like Jesus, because of your strong relationship with God, you'll be able to humble yourself and be authentic with your spouse.

Emotional intimacy doesn't have to be limited to fairy tales and made-for-TV marriages. It can be a reality in every marriage, including yours. But the environment required to cultivate emotional safety and therefore yield relational authenticity must be fiercely protected. Once trust and emotional security have been lost, they can take years to regain. So pray. Pray for God to make your home a loving incubator for relational vulnerability. Pray that you'll always react to your spouse in a godly, humble fashion, even when it's difficult. Pray for your marriage to be the safest place on earth for both of you.

Pray Big Today

Here are some ways to help produce intimacy in your marriage:

- Pray about your relationship with God. Pray that you'll feel totally free and secure before him. Pray that your relationship with God will be the most important and meaningful one in your life. Pray the same for your spouse.
- Pray for authenticity before God. Confess your sins and your deepest fears and feelings to him. Don't hide from him.
- Pray every day *for* your spouse. Pray that he or she will be real and authentic before God.
- If possible, pray every day *with* your spouse. If one of you is out of town, pray over the phone. Always pray together at night before you go to sleep.
- Ask God to show you where you're being inauthentic in marriage. Pray for the opportunity and courage to really be "naked" before your spouse.
- Pray that your marriage will be the safe and authentic place that God intends it to be.
- Pray that God will give you and your spouse the gift of emotional intimacy.

Verses about Emotional Intimacy to Pray for Your Marriage

- Genesis 2:24–25: *Father, I pray that my spouse and I will forsake other sources of human dependency and cleave to each other every day. Make us one—the way you intended a marriage relationship to be. I pray also, Lord, that you will give us the courage, grace, and love to be relationally naked before each other without shame. Please make us safe places for each other.*

- Ephesians 4:15: *Holy Father, give us the commitment and the courage to always tell each other the truth, and to do so in love.*
- Ephesians 4:29: *Precious God, protect us from speaking evil, mean, or unwholesome words to each other. Train us to speak only those words that build each other up and that encourage intimacy.*

A Marriage Pinpoint Prayer

Precious Father, thank you for the gift of intimacy. Thank you for dying to make it possible for me to have intimacy with you. Please be the most important relationship in my life. Help me to love you, desire you, and need you more than anyone or anything else. I pray for my marriage. Help my spouse and me to be secure enough in you that we can be authentic with each other. Make us like Jesus—knowing where we came from and where we are going—so that we can humble ourselves, wash each other's feet, and share even our deepest hurts and fears. Give us, O God, Eden-level intimacy. I pray this for us in Jesus's holy name. Amen.

5

PRAYING FOR
SPIRITUAL INTIMACY

THAT'S WHY I think couples should always have sex before they get too serious. I mean, if they can't have great sex, what's the point of staying together?" The guy who sat before me in my office was quite serious, but I couldn't believe what I was hearing. According to him, men and women need to be as sexually active as possible before marriage. His mind-set was, "Find a girl who is great in bed and hang on to her. What's the point of marrying a sexual dud? If I'm going to have to live with somebody for the rest of my life, I might as well have great sex in the process. Right?"

I hear statements like that far too often. After stomaching as much of this relational gibberish as I can, I typically ask, "What if your wife has a car wreck early on in your marriage, is paralyzed from the neck down, and can never be sexual again? Are you going to be okay with that?" My question usually draws a long, awkward pause from Casanova as he considers the right response. It's especially fun to ask this question in front of his current sexual partner.

Culture has sold most men and women, including Christ-followers, a major bill of goods. It has convinced us that sexual intimacy is the highest form of relational oneness. Sexual expression is the intimacy level that most couples default to and stop at. Many couples (married, engaged, dating, and/or living together) gauge the success or health of their relationship by the frequency and "wow factor" of their sex. But in reality, the sexual union may be the lowest and most easily attained level of relational intimacy. God created sex and wants it to be enjoyed in the proper relational context. But there is clearly more implied in the description of naked-without-shame intimacy that we looked at in the last chapter. Sex, regardless of our culture's obsession with it, is not the end-all in a relationship.

I believe that spiritual intimacy is the highest level of intimacy two people can enjoy. Friendships, small group relationships, and especially marriages reach their highest and most profound levels of intimacy when they prioritize and work toward spiritual oneness. Everything about us that is physical will pass away. Physical intimacy is wonderful and God-given, but it's not the highest level of intimacy that humans can experience. Relationships that push toward spiritual forms of intimacy will reach spheres of unity, love, and authenticity that far exceed and outlast any physical expression of tenderness and care. In other words, *if you want to be truly intimate with someone, get to know their soul.*[1]

One Heart and One Way

There is a great promise in Jeremiah 24:7 that you can pray as you seek spiritual intimacy in your marriage. It states, "I will give them a heart to know Me, for I am the LORD; and they will be My people, and I will be their God, for they will return to Me with their whole heart" (NASB).

Susie and I discovered the power of this promise when we were in college. We were in a particularly difficult season in our relationship. I wasn't sure if we should continue dating. I wanted to know if our relationship had the potential to become a great marriage. I remember sitting on my bed late one night and randomly opening my Bible. It fell open to Jeremiah 24. Verse 7 immediately jumped off the page at me. What struck me about this great promise to the nation of Israel was the single form of the word *heart* that Jeremiah used. Given that God was speaking to a multitude of people, I would have expected the text to say *hearts*, not *heart*. But God was promising to resurrect his people from exile and to seal and mark them with his presence. Therefore, they would be his people; he would be their God. As a nation, they would have one heart and one soul.

That profound concept—that a group of people could have one heart—grabbed my attention. I immediately sensed that God was offering this promise to me and Susie. If we would be his people—if we would seek him, honor him, and serve him—then he would be our God. He would guide us as a couple and would give us *one heart* for him. That day I started praying Jeremiah 24:7 for our relationship. I shared the verse with Susie, and she began praying it as well. Together we've asked God on thousands of occasions to give us one heart for him.

Over the years, Susie and I have grown more and more unified in our commitment to Christ. We've watched each other settle into our respective walks with Jesus, and that has had a profound impact on how we relate as a couple. We have the privilege (by God's grace) of relating on a level that many couples never choose to experience. It's not that they can't; they just don't. The level of intimacy that Susie and I enjoy is available to every Christian couple who will seek it from God. It's a gift of God's grace and the fruit of years of Jeremiah 24:7–type praying. It's the intimacy that happens between two humans on a spiritual level—the intimacy of two human souls.

Praying Jeremiah 24:7

Put the promise of Jeremiah 24:7 to work in your marriage. Add the language of this great verse to your regular prayers for you and your spouse. Here's the verse again: "I will give them a heart to know Me, for I am the LORD; and they will be My people, and I will be their God, for they will return to Me with their whole heart" (NASB).

- Pray that God will give you and your spouse one heart. Pray that you'll be on the same page when it comes to your relationship with God.
- Pray for spiritual intimacy. Ask God to create an environment conducive to true spiritual authenticity.
- Pray that you and your spouse will both know the Lord. Pray for moments of spiritual insight, spiritual conversations, and joint worship in your marriage.
- Pray every day that God will be the Lord of your marriage. Name yourselves as his people. Claim him daily as your God.
- Pray that you and your spouse will constantly seek his presence and power in your marriage.
- Pray for protection from distractions and temporal tangents that would keep you and your spouse from seeking God. Pray that you'll seek him with your whole heart.

Now that you know how to pray for one heart, let's look at the power and beauty of spiritual intimacy.

Pray Big Prayer Starter

Ask God to give you a specific verse of Scripture to pray for your marriage. Pray that he will use his Word to show you what specifically to pray for your marriage.

The Benefits of Spiritual Intimacy

While spiritual intimacy is clearly a biblical concept, it is implied in the Bible rather than stated directly. Let's think about the important features of this great gift of spiritual oneness.

Spiritual intimacy is the highest form of relational connection, and it is the most difficult to develop. Let's get this point settled early on—spiritual intimacy is the most intense, most satisfying, most rewarding, and longest-lasting form of a relational connection two people can have. It's also the most difficult to establish. Those who intend to connect spiritually have to work at it. They have to pray about it and seek God's guidance and assistance in the aligning of their souls.

Spiritual intimacy connects your soul—your innermost being, the essence of who you are—with a peer's, and it does so around a set of values that are nonnegotiable and unchanging. Spiritual intimacy is a precursor to the kind of unimaginable relational fulfillment we will all experience in heaven. There we will be able to relate to others on a profound and eternal level unmatched on earth. Without the encumbrances of sin, flesh, and emotional inhibitions, we will instantly be known and be able to know others fully. Those who do the hard work of pursuing a spiritual connection with their spouse help to create spiritual moments in their households that are divine samplings of what we will know in eternity. Spiritual intimacy is worth the effort, hard work, and prayers required to create it. It really is a little bit of heaven on earth. And it's what God wants for your marriage.

Spiritual intimacy begins with a mutual commitment to Christ. We discussed this at length in chapter 3, so I'll only briefly reiterate it here. For you to know true spiritual intimacy with your spouse, you both have to love Jesus more than you love each other. Married followers of Christ who have fully yielded their lives to him have taken the first and most important step toward a true spiritual connection. Your Jesus-first mind-set enables you as a couple to pursue something bigger than yourselves. It moves you to see beyond your own wants and needs in marriage. It places you both in proper perspective before each other and before God.

When you function in your marriage as two surrendered and yielded adults, it levels the playing field in your relationship. Your yieldedness to Christ communicates that you are on the same page on the most important issue of all—who or what you worship as God. Such mutual surrender to Christ paves the way for you to connect spiritually with your spouse.

Spiritual intimacy grows out of a mutual commitment to each other. The Christian gospel boasts of the unconditional love and favor of God. Recipients of God's grace know that his love for them is without exception or limit and is completely undeserved. Christ-followers know they are living in and enjoying the amazing lopsided favor of God's love.[2] They also know that they are called to model that love in their relationships with each other. There is no better relationship than marriage for modeling God's unconditional love.

When you adopt God's love as the standard for your marriage, it opens the door for deep levels of spiritual intimacy. When you are committed to each other and will love each other no matter what, you create the fertile soil of trust from which true spiritual intimacy grows. You share spiritual struggles, victories, and vision. You encourage each other in your respective spiritual efforts. You pray for and support each other. You become teammates, not competitors.

Spiritual intimacy requires mutual willingness to be spiritually authentic. Steve is struggling in his job again. It's not that he's underperforming; he's actually a highly valued employee. It's just that he's not happy. This is Steve's fourth job in seven years. He's never been fired or asked to leave. He's just not happy. Steve's patient wife, Sarah, has stuck with him through all his career chaos. His frequent job changes have cost them financially and have greatly impaired her sense of security. Their marriage isn't perfect, but it is still intimate.

Steve and Sarah have made it a practice to be honest with each other. When Steve feels aimless in his job, he tells Sarah. He seeks her input and prayers as he wrestles with his life's direction. When Sarah feels tired, frustrated, or insecure because of Steve's lack of direction, she confesses it to him. They pray together and determine to seek God's direction, provision, and leadership for their future.

How could a couple not grow closer in that type of environment? In a home where each spouse feels the freedom to openly discuss their spiritual struggles and where spiritual conversations happen on a regular basis, spiritual intimacy will be the inevitable result. Do you and your spouse talk about spiritual matters? Do you both feel the freedom to be authentic about your spiritual concerns? Ask God to give you such a marriage environment. It will breed the kind of intimacy that God wants you to know.

Pray Big Prayer Starter

Pray that you and your spouse will be hungry for real spiritual intimacy. Pray that you won't settle for or slip into the rut of being spiritually inauthentic. Pray for the ability to talk about your respective relationships with God in loving, honest, and encouraging ways.

Being Spiritual Partners

Let me introduce you to one of my favorite couples in the Bible—Priscilla and Aquila. These New Testament heroes had a high-impact marriage. Both were Jewish converts to Christianity who had met the apostle Paul in the city of Corinth. They befriended him and became colaborers with him in ministry.

In Acts 18, Luke tells us how God used their marriage to help a new believer named Apollos:

> Meanwhile a Jew named Apollos, a native of Alexandria, came to Ephesus. He was a learned man, with a thorough knowledge of the Scriptures. He had been instructed in the way of the Lord, and he spoke with great fervor and taught about Jesus accurately, though he knew only the baptism of John. He began to speak boldly in the synagogue. When Priscilla and Aquila heard him, they invited him to their home and explained to him the way of God more adequately.
>
> Acts 18:24–26

Priscilla and Aquila's impact on Apollos was dramatic. After his time with them, Apollos became even more effective. Luke writes, "He vigorously refuted the Jews in public debate, proving from the Scriptures that Jesus was the Christ" (v. 28). God used the ministry of this married couple to help train one of the great early Christian evangelists.

Paul mentions Priscilla and Aquila several times in his letters, and he always mentions both of them. He also names Priscilla before Aquila, which was unheard of in Jewish culture. Women were typically referenced *after* men. This tells us that Paul had great respect for both of them as Christ-followers. It also tells us that they both were very spiritually mature.

How many couples do you know who are not even close to being at the same level spiritually? Frequently one spouse is very mature and the other, though a Christian, appears to be stuck in spiritual preadolescence. That can make for tough going in a marriage, and it's a major hindrance to spiritual intimacy.

Use Priscilla and Aquila as an example of the kind of couple you want to be. Pray that you and your spouse will be at the same stage of spiritual development. Pray that you'll both love Bible reading, prayer, and worship. Pray that your marriage will impact others. Ask God to give both of you strong Christian communities where you can be accountable and be encouraged. Pray that God will help you both to stay spiritually stimulated and growing. Don't settle for a spiritual mismatch. Pray that you'll grow up together spiritually, like Priscilla and Aquila.

Hebrews 6:1 says, "Therefore let us leave the elementary teachings about Christ and go on to maturity." Pray this verse for your marriage. Ask God to lead both you and your spouse into spiritual maturity. Pray that neither of you would be stuck in the spiritual basics. Ask God to give both of you the desire to grow into spiritual maturity.

Pray Big Prayer Starter

Pray that you and your spouse will excel spiritually. Pray that you both will love God with all your heart, soul, mind, and strength.

71

The Most Intimate Marriage Act

Believe it or not, the most intimate act a married couple can engage in is prayer.

Jesus promises that when two or more gather together in his name, he will meet with them (see Matt. 18:20). That's an amazing promise given to groups of believers of any size. Even if just two of us meet together in Jesus's name, he promises to be there with us.

What would happen if you and your spouse regularly met together in Jesus's name? What if you made prayer a part of everything you did? I mean praying not just *for* each other but *with* each other. How would your budget discussions be different if you prayed together about your resources before you talked about them? How would talks that grew into arguments go differently if you paused to pray together before you started sharing your feelings? What view would your children have of prayer (and marriage) if you constantly prayed together with them? How would your romantic life be different if you prayed together regularly for passionate, selfless love? Prayer in marriage is a potent and unlimited intimacy booster.

Susie and I learned the power of praying as a couple early in our relationship. We made praying together a habit, even on our first date. (Susie was the godliest girl I had ever known. I knew she would dump me in an instant if I didn't pray with her!) We used to pray that God would break us up if we ever became too focused on each other or if our relationship ever stopped honoring him. And we learned (painfully) that God was quite willing to answer those prayers. As a married couple, we've seen God answer countless pinpoint prayers for our relationship, our children, our ministries, our finances, our health, and our respective walks with him. As we've been willing to pray for our marriage, God has proven to be more than willing to answer our prayers with his power.

You can know his power too. Make prayer a part of everything you do as a couple. It will teach you to bare your soul before your spouse. It will show you how to talk about everything—large and small—with each other and with God. And most of all, it will lead you as a couple into the holy presence of God. That's the greatest intimacy builder of all.

I know that some of you who have never prayed together as a couple think this sounds very scary and imposing. It doesn't have to be. Here are a few tips for praying together well:

- Talk about it first. If you're not sure what to do, decide beforehand which of you will start and finish the prayer.
- Hold hands and close your eyes. It will keep distractions out and make you feel more connected.
- Keep it short. Long praying is not the same as effective praying. Don't try to pray for a certain amount of time. Just say what's on your heart, even if it lasts only for a few seconds.
- Don't preach or criticize. Do not say something like, "Lord, please help my pagan-swine spouse to quit being such a jerk!" Pray for God's favor, encouragement, and anointing on your spouse's life. If he or she needs to be convicted about something, let God do it. It's not your job.
- Thank God for his blessings. Expressing gratitude in prayer is a great way to unify your hearts and gain perspective on your marriage. Be sure to thank him for all he has done for you.

Pray Big Today

Here are some additional ways to make prayer a part of your marriage routine:

- Pray together before meals.
- Pray together at night before you go to sleep.
- Pray together in the morning before you start your day.
- If you have children, pray together with them.
- Pray with and for your spouse when he or she is hurting or struggling through something.
- Pray together before you begin a serving project.
- Pray together about important decisions.
- Pray together before you write your tithe check to your church. Ask God to receive it as your act of worship.

Verses to Pray for Your Spiritual Intimacy

- Matthew 18:20: *Father, as my spouse and I meet together in your name, please be here with us. See us as your submitted people. As we draw near to you, Lord Jesus, draw near to us.*
- John 17:21: *Lord Jesus, I pray for my marriage as you prayed for your followers: make us one. Let our unity and spiritual intimacy reflect the love and commitment that exists between you and your Father.*
- Ephesians 1:17: *Holy God, please give my spouse and me a spirit of wisdom and revelation so that we might continually know you better.*

74

A Marriage Pinpoint Prayer

Holy Father, you are my God. You are my spouse's God. We have both yielded our lives to you. Because of that, please give us one heart. Give us unity, openness, and intimacy on a spiritual level. I pray that my spouse and I would be spiritually mature. Help us to love your Word, love prayer, love worship and serving, and hate sin. I also pray that my spouse and I will both continue to grow up spiritually. Please continue your holy work in us. Help us to never settle spiritually for less than you intended. Give us the spiritual relationship with each other that you want us to have. I ask this in Jesus's name. Amen.

6

YIELD RIGHT OF WAY

I WAS HAVING SUCH a great ride. It's a shame it had to end early.

I was in the twenty-fifth mile of a forty-mile bike trek in the hills west of Austin. It was Monday, April 16, 2001, the day after Easter. As part of my recovery from a full Easter weekend, I had scheduled in a few extra hours for a long ride. I was hoping for a beautiful day and an invigorating ride. I wasn't disappointed. The spring weather in Austin was gorgeous, and I was "in the zone" on my bike. The ride was going well, and I was aiming for a personal best time on the challenging, hill-intensive course I'd chosen.

As I zoomed down a long hill, I leaned forward in a tuck position to get as much speed as possible. I was cruising along at close to thirty miles per hour when I saw a silver flash in front of me. It was a Mitsubishi Gallant. The car's seventeen-year-old driver hadn't seen me and had turned left, pulling directly in front of me. I remember seeing the car, squeezing my brakes, hearing glass shatter, feeling two

77

violent jerks, and then finding myself on the pavement with terrible pain in my right hip.

I had hit the car in the right rear passenger door, my bike shattering the door's window. My head apparently bounced along and dented the car's roof before I went airborne. According to witnesses, I did two or three cartwheels in the air before landing in a heap about forty feet from the point of impact. The crash landing basically filleted my hip.

After promising the young and terrified driver that I wouldn't sue him (my dad, an attorney, said that I was obviously in a state of shock and couldn't be held responsible for that promise), I urged him to call 911. I was placed in a neck brace and immobilized, then taken by ambulance to the hospital as a Level II trauma patient. The paramedics were concerned about internal injuries and bleeding, as well as head and neck injuries. My injuries turned out to be limited to countless cuts and scrapes (a piece of glass popped out of my leg six months after the wreck) and a rather large hole in my hip. I give God, a few dozen angels, and a good helmet the credit for my relatively unscathed condition.

The real injury, however, was to Susie. It's hard to explain the trauma involved in getting a call from a paramedic about your spouse. Susie was told that I had been hit but that I was okay. She was told to meet the ambulance at the emergency room. She obviously wasn't prepared for what she saw—her husband in a neck brace, bloodied head to toe in a tattered bike jersey and shorts, strapped to a gurney, and hooked up to an IV. Let's just say that it didn't create a lot of confidence for Susie in my cycling skills or in the safety of the sport I loved so much. When she saw me, she immediately hoped and prayed that I would never get on a bike again.

I, on the other hand, was calculating just how nice of a new bike I could get with the insurance settlement. And that, of course, led to conflict.

Learning to Yield

What should you do when each spouse in a marriage feels equally strong about an opposing point of view? How do you resolve the conflict? In our case, Susie made a decision that humbled me and that I still admire—she yielded. She shared how she felt, prayed that God would give me wisdom to make the right decision, and then told me to do what I thought was right. It was an incredibly mature response on her part, and one that made me think long and hard about my decision to get back on a bike.

So what happened? I bought a top-of-the-line bike with the money we got from insurance. On my first ride after being hit, I had two very close calls with cars. Plus the sight of pavement whizzing by at twenty miles per hour actually made me nauseated. (Susie has never actually confessed to praying for this speed-induced nausea, but I remain suspicious.) I returned the bike to the shop and got my money back. Then I stopped riding. I haven't ridden since, and God has honored the decision.

"You Go First." "No, You Go First." "No, Really, I Insist—You Go First."

If you've been around the church very long or spent much time reading the Bible, you've probably encountered Paul's teachings on marriage in Ephesians 5. To the men of Ephesus he wrote, "Husbands, love your wives, just as Christ loved the church and gave himself up for her" (Eph. 5:25). And to the women, "Wives, submit to your husbands as to the Lord" (v. 22). I've always thought it interesting that the command to women gets much more airtime and pulpit attention than the command to men. Maybe it's because most pulpits are filled by men. Or it may be because of Paul's use of the notorious *s* word—*submit*.

There is no doubt that these two commands, and especially the one to women, are frequently quoted, misquoted, and misapplied. But I wonder if you've ever noticed or been taught the significance of the verse that immediately precedes Paul's teachings on marriage in Ephesians: "Submit to one another out of reverence for Christ" (v. 21). I'm going to be mentioning this verse frequently in the rest of the chapter, so you might as well go ahead and commit the verse to memory. Here it is again: "Submit to one another out of reverence for Christ."

Let's consider where this verse is placed in the writer's flow of thought. Look at Ephesians 5:17–20: "Therefore do not be foolish, but understand what the Lord's will is. Do not get drunk on wine, which leads to debauchery. Instead, be filled with the Spirit. Speak to one another with psalms, hymns and spiritual songs. Sing and make music in your heart to the Lord, always giving thanks to God the Father for everything, in the name of our Lord Jesus Christ."

In these verses, Paul instructs believers about the impact that following Christ should have on our lives. He gives a few broad commands for each of us to adhere to. First, he tells us to understand what God's will is for our lives. Second, he commands us to be filled with God's Holy Spirit. If we're filled with his Spirit, we'll live, love, and serve as we're supposed to. Third, Paul commands us to speak biblical truth to each other and have worshipful, grateful hearts.

After offering these instructions, the apostle is ready to talk about our roles in marriage. Instead of jumping right into the marriage topic, however, Paul adds a critical transition statement. Under the guidance of the Holy Spirit, Paul masterfully sums up the teachings he's just given and at the same time introduces the topic he wants to move into. Here again is his majestic statement: "Submit to one another out of reverence for Christ."

With five simple Greek words, Paul gives a command that levels the playing field for all Christians. It applies to masters and slaves, parents and children, employers and employees, executives and custodians, men and women, husbands and wives. Paul didn't hesitate to teach about the respective roles we have in life and in following Christ, or about the lines of authority that God establishes in our relationships, but he wanted those roles to be understood in light of his command to yield to each other in love.

Let's establish a simple, working definition of the principle of mutual submission that Paul espouses in Christian relationships: *Yielding is deliberately placing someone else's needs before your own, seeing someone else as more important than you, and seeking someone else's benefit over yours.* Mutual submission occurs when each Christ-follower in a relationship or group chooses to yield to the needs of the others.

Applied to marriage, mutual submission is preferring, honoring, exalting, and promoting your spouse over yourself. It's seeing your spouse's needs and wants as more important than your own. And, by the way, it's nearly impossible to do consistently without prayer.

Pray Big Prayer Starter

Pray for a humble heart toward your spouse.
Ask God to help you to joyfully place
him or her ahead of yourself.

A Hot Topic

I was in the sauna recently, talking to a personal trainer who works at the place where I exercise. We've become friends over the years. He frequently gives me free workout tips (he can see the need when he looks at me), and I frequently give him spiritual counsel. Our recent encounter was no exception. After my friend offered me some tips on how to improve my swim workout, I asked about his marriage. He told me about a business venture his wife was considering. He was afraid it wouldn't be successful and that they would lose money on the deal. He then asked what I thought. After asking a few exploratory questions, I gave my friend this counsel: "Tell her your concerns. Be authentic with her, and then yield. Support her decision fully. And if the venture fails, don't say, 'I told you so.'"

Can mutual submission really work in marriage? Can men and women really learn to defer to each other out of their reverence for Christ? Are there times when husbands or wives need to yield to their spouses, even though it doesn't fully make sense to them? The answer to each of these questions, according to the Bible, is a resounding *yes!* Mutual deference doesn't cancel out our marriage roles and certainly isn't always easy. But when it is at work in a marriage, it can produce increased love and trust between spouses and increase the couple's collective faith in God.

Pray Big Prayer Starter

Pray for enough faith to let God deal with
the implications of your spouse's
decisions, including the bad ones.

Mutual Submission in Marriage

Are you intrigued? Does the concept of mutual submission sound appealing to you for your marriage? How would your relationship be different if you and your spouse prayed

Ephesians 5:21 every day for your marriage? Are you ready to start praying for you and your spouse to be mutually yielded to each other?

Let's look at what yielding in marriage is and what it isn't so we can pray more effectively about it. We'll start with what mutual submission isn't.

Mutual submission isn't a "you win, I lose" concept. There's no winning or losing when believers defer to each other. Jesus didn't lose when he obeyed the Father, submitted himself to our needs, and died for our sins. Obedience is never losing. Yielding to your spouse in marriage isn't losing or giving up. It's obedience to God. When we're obedient to God's leadership, everyone wins.

Mutual submission isn't an "I have no value" confession. Yielding in marriage isn't a cowering concession to the superior spouse. It doesn't flow out of low self-esteem and a "doormat" mind-set. Yielding is the loving choice to elevate your mate and to lower yourself. It has nothing to do with one spouse's position or rank over the other.

Mutual submission isn't a "you're right and I'm wrong" admission. While there are certainly times in marriage when we need to admit our guilt or error and seek the forgiveness of our spouse, that is not the same as choosing to yield in a matter. A deferring spouse can feel quite strongly about his or her side of an issue and still choose to yield. Yielding in marriage doesn't require a right or wrong verdict. It's rather a question of who God thinks should defer in a given situation.

When I wanted to buy the new bike, Susie felt very strongly that I should never ride again. Those feelings were logical and very justified. When she chose to yield to me anyway, over and against her better judgment, she wasn't saying that she agreed with me. She was acknowledging that God was leading her to defer in that particular instance.

Mutual submission isn't a forced acquiescence to another's will. I need to be very clear about this. Many women have been led to believe that they're supposed to submit to their husband no matter what. They've been taught that submission means tolerating verbal, physical, or sexual abuse, not "griping" about their husband's pornography or strip-club habit, or just "forgiving" his philandering lifestyle. Submission isn't that. Wives who put up with such irresponsible behavior from the husbands are, in fact, enabling them and actually contributing to their dysfunctional lifestyle. To look the other way while your husband destroys himself and your marriage is to quietly condone his sin, deny God's Word in your life, and devalue who you are in Christ.

I'm not giving you permission here to march down to the courthouse and file for divorce. Far from it. I'm rather encouraging you to require your husband to live by the basic standards of acceptable behavior in a Christian marriage. If he can't or won't, then get the help of a pastor or Christian counselor and figure out how to confront your husband lovingly about his unacceptable behavior. Submitting as a wife or simply yielding as a Christian spouse has nothing to do with fear, intimidation, threats, or tolerating inexcusable and ungodly behavior.

Mutual submission doesn't look for payback. There is no reciprocity in yielding. Even though both spouses are commanded to yield, you should yield whether your spouse does or not. Let God deal with your spouse concerning his or her lack of obedience to him. Submit because it's right, biblical, and what God expects. Look for ways to yield to your spouse whether he or she deserves it or not.

Now that we've seen what mutual submission isn't, let's zero in on what it is.

Mutual submission is willingly setting aside your own desires to meet the needs of your spouse. Yielding is a love gift in marriage. It's offered because you love Christ and want to honor your mate. When you defer, you show your spouse that loving and serving him or her at that moment is more important than meeting your own needs or promoting your own agenda.

Mutual submission is choosing to walk in unity with your spouse rather than asserting your own way. When you yield, you know that you don't always have to be right. You can choose to defer to your spouse simply because the issue at hand isn't worth fighting over. When possible, unity is a much better choice than conflict. Deferring shows your spouse that you're willing to not always get your way.

Mutual submission is choosing to set aside what's best for you and choosing what's best for your marriage. Yielding has a "What's best for us?" mind-set. At times, you'll be led to yield for the good of the marriage, not just for the good of your spouse.

I had the chance to do this recently in my marriage. Susie and our kids were all going to be out of town over spring break. Our church was taking a mission trip to Mississippi that same week, and I really wanted to go. However, Susie was hoping I would stay in Austin and "mind the fort." You know, keep an eye on the house and take care of the bird, cat, and two dogs we call family. I'm a much cheaper option than paying a house sitter. I can tell you, there was no contest on how I wanted to spend my time. I love missions and have close relationships with the people we were going to serve. But in this case, what was best for *me* wasn't best for *us*, so I yielded. I stayed home with the Davis critters. It was the right thing for me to do.

Mutual submission is choosing not to exert rank or authority when you could. This one is especially important for all you husbands who think submission means you have the final say in every marriage issue. Just because your role

85

may place you in authority over your family and make you accountable to God for your family's spiritual well-being, that doesn't mean you have the right to flex your leadership muscles in every marriage circumstance. The beauty and power of mutual submission is that rank and entitlement go out the window and are replaced with love, a desire to serve the other, and humility.

A Prayer That Will Change Your Marriage

Are you ready to begin praying the Ephesians 5:21 command for your marriage? More specifically, would you be willing to begin praying it just for yourself, regardless of how your spouse acts? Praying this verse can have a profound impact on your marriage. Here are some things to pray when seeking a mutually submitted marriage:

- *Pray for the Holy Spirit's filling.* Continually ask God to fill both you and your spouse with his Spirit (see Eph. 5:18). As you increasingly yield to and are subsequently filled with Jesus's Spirit, it will become more natural for you to defer to your spouse in marriage.
- *Pray for a willing spirit.* Mutual submission is supposed to be voluntary, not forced, coerced, or even reluctant. Griping while deferring doesn't count! Pray that you can yield joyfully and readily.
- *Pray that both you and your spouse will revere Christ.* Mutual submission is motivated by our desire to honor and love Jesus. We don't yield to our spouses because they've earned it or because we think they will reciprocate. We yield to honor Jesus. We defer to others because Christ deferred to us. Any unwillingness to

yield to your spouse when Jesus is leading you to is a sign of a breakdown in your obedience to Christ. Pray that you and your spouse will practice instant obedience and willingly yield to the needs of the other.

Pray Big Prayer Starter

Pray Ephesians 5:18–20 for your marriage—*Lord, help us not to be drunk with wine but to be filled with your Holy Spirit. Teach us to speak to each other with psalms, hymns, and spiritual songs, to sing and make music in our hearts to you, and to always give you thanks for everything in the name of our Lord Jesus Christ.*

Praying for Downward Mobility

Once again, our best example of how to act in marriage comes from the Lord Jesus. He is the ultimate role model for deferring to our spouses. Consider these inspired words:

Your attitude should be the same as that of Christ Jesus: Who, being in very nature God, did not consider equality with God something to be grasped, but made himself nothing, taking the very nature of a servant, being made in human likeness. And being found in appearance as a man, he humbled himself and became obedient to death—even death on a cross! Therefore God exalted him to the highest place and gave him the name that is above every name, that at the name of Jesus every knee should bow, in heaven and on earth and under the earth, and every tongue confess that Jesus Christ is Lord, to the glory of God the Father.

Philippians 2:5–11

This passage paints a picture of Jesus emptying himself of all his rights and divine privileges so he could become human. He set aside deity and embraced humanity so he could die—specifically, so he could die for you and me. There is no better example of one person yielding to another. Did you catch Paul's opening comment in the passage above? "Your attitude should be the same as that of Christ Jesus." He tells us that we should treat others the same way Jesus treats us. He commands us to empty ourselves of our supposed rights and yield as Jesus did.

There is no better place to practice having the mind-set of Jesus than in marriage. Pray for an attitude like Jesus's. Pray that you will willingly become less important (see John 3:30). Ask God to help you set aside what you perceive your rights and privileges to be and to think about your spouse the way Jesus thinks about you. Pray for a humble heart and a yielding spirit.

Pray Big Today

- Pray for opportunities to place your spouse's choices and needs before your own.
- Pray for ways to serve your mate. Ask God to give you opportunities to wash his or her feet.
- Pray that you will respect and esteem your spouse. Pray for ways to affirm him or her, both publicly and privately.
- Pray for appropriate and healthy desires for your spouse. Pray for a willingness to meet his or her physical and sexual needs.
- Ask God to help you see your spouse as a gift from God. Pray that you will freely embrace your spouse as God's creation and accept who God is making him or her to be in Christ. Pray for ways to show your spouse that you love and accept him or her unconditionally.

- Pray every day for your mate. Intercede for his or her health, prosperity, relationship with Christ, career, and relationship with you.

Verses about Yielding to Pray for Your Marriage

- Ephesians 5:21: *Father, I pray that my spouse and I will submit to each other out of reverence for you.*
- Romans 15:2: *Lord, help us to promote the good of the other and to build each other up.*
- Philippians 2:3–4: *Father, I pray that I would do nothing out of selfish ambition or vain conceit but in humility consider my spouse better than myself. Help me to look not only to my own interests but also to my spouse's.*

A Marriage Pinpoint Prayer

Holy Father, I love you and praise you. Thank you for my wife. Thank you for gifting her to me. Thank you for placing her in my life so that I might serve her, affirm her, and embrace her freely. Help me to treat her as you treat me. God, please give me the gift of downward mobility. Show me how to defer to my wife, yield to her, and submit to her. Please shatter my pride and my need to always be right. Give me discernment to know when to defer to my wife in decisions and choices that affect our lives. Help me to look for ways to serve her and to elevate her over myself. Teach me, precious Savior, to submit to her out of reverence for you. I pray this in Jesus's holy name. Amen.

7

How to Pray for Your Husband

Jim and Nell Hamm, married just two weeks shy of fifty years, were enjoying one of their frequent day hikes in Prairie Creek Redwoods State Park in northern California. Jim, age seventy, and Nell, age sixty-five, found hiking to be a great way to enjoy each other's company and exercise at the same time. But on January 28, 2007, their routine outing turned tragic. A young mountain lion suddenly and viciously attacked Jim, locking his head in its mouth. Nell, keeping her wits about her, grabbed a nearby log and began beating the animal on the head. When that had no apparent effect on the lion, Nell grabbed Jim's ballpoint pen from his pocket and began jabbing it in the animal's eye. She struck the cat with such force that the pen actually broke in two, but the enraged animal still wouldn't release its death grip on Jim. As a last resort, Nell again grabbed the log and attacked the cat. After several minutes of intense battle, the cat let go of Jim, gave Nell a long stare, and then turned and walked away.

Jim survived the attack, and Nell was hailed as a hero and credited with saving her husband's life. Jim, recuperating from his hospital bed, spoke of his wife's courage: "She stood in there the whole time. If she hadn't, I would be gone. . . . No doubt about it . . . I'd be gone." Nell was quick to dismiss claims of any heroic action on her part: "You hear remarks of hero," she said. "It wasn't that. We love each other very much . . . and we just fought together like we do everything."[1]

Ladies, in this chapter, I'm asking you to fight for your husband. I'm asking you to go to battle against the powers in our culture that are well positioned to devastate men's lives. I'm asking you not to be naive about what your husband struggles with every day and to rally to his side. I want you to gain a vision of the kind of man your husband can become. I want you to pray for a picture of what God intends for your husband and then to pray for that picture to become a reality in his life. I'm asking you to become your man's number one fan, supporter, believer, and, most important, intercessor. You can't change your husband; prayer can.

Pick a Hero and Pray

Praying for your husband doesn't have to be difficult. The Bible is loaded with great examples of men whom you can pray your husband will imitate. Just find biblical characters who manifested the godly and holy traits you desire to see in your husband's life, and then start praying for your husband to have the same characteristics. Use the Scriptures as your guide.

Does your husband need more faith? Pray through Hebrews 11 and ask God to give him the faith of Noah,

Abraham, or Moses. Does he need to be more obedient? Pray that he'll be like Peter, Andrew, James, and John, who dropped their nets and immediately obeyed Jesus's call (see Matt. 4:18–22). Is your husband unfamiliar with the Bible? Pray that he will be like Apollos, whom Luke described as "mighty in the Scriptures" (Acts 18:24 NASB).

Pray for your husband to have Solomon's wisdom (see 1 Kings 3:10–12) and Jeremiah's courage (see Jer. 1:17–19). Pray that he will be as bold as Paul (see Eph. 6:19–20) and as generous as Barnabas (see Acts 4:36–37). Ask God to give your husband a passion like David's, who was a man after God's own heart (see 1 Sam. 13:14). As you get more familiar with the concepts of pinpoint praying and praying the Scriptures, you can find other biblical characters and pray that your husband might imitate them.

Pray Big Prayer Starter

Pray 1 Chronicles 12:8 (NASB) for your husband—
Lord, please make my husband a mighty man of God.

Your Husband's Best Role Model

You're never going to do any better than Jesus. Without exception, he is the best example of a loving, caring husband. In the same way that Jesus loves, leads, and serves his bride, the church, pray that your husband will love, lead, and serve you. Don't pray this just for your benefit. Your husband will be more fruitful and fulfilled as he obeys God's calling on his life. Pray that his joy may be complete as he leads, loves, and serves you the way that Jesus does.

Your husband isn't perfect. He's not going to be the flawless person Jesus is. But he can be Christlike. So pray that your man will be like Jesus as he functions in his God-given role as your husband. Let's look at the perfect example of Jesus and see how you can pray powerful pinpoint prayers for your man.

In his lofty passage on the roles of husbands and wives in Ephesians 5, the apostle Paul commanded husbands to love their wives in the same way that Jesus loves the church (see v. 25). Paul presented Jesus as the ultimate example of a loving and caring husband and instructed husbands to set their sights on Jesus as their marriage role model. In light of this command, here are some pinpoint prayers that you can pray for your husband as he seeks to fulfill his God-given assignment.

Pray that he will be a great intercessor. Jesus was a man of prayer. In fact, he was the greatest role model for prayer who ever lived. You might think that it was easy for Jesus to live a godly life and love sinners because he was God's Son. But in reality, everything Jesus did—love, forgive, heal, teach, lead, and change the world—he did as a fully submitted human. Prayer made the difference for Jesus. He lived an anointed life by the power of God's Spirit in him, and he fueled the fire of God's Spirit through prayer. If you want your man to live like Jesus, ask God to help him learn to pray like Jesus.

Hebrews 7:25 tells us that Jesus is praying for us right now in heaven. He is always interceding before his Father on our behalf. He prays for us because he loves us and sees prayer as part of his duty as a loving husband. I love knowing that my Savior lives to intercede and seek God's best for me. I love knowing that he loves me enough to pray for me. Would you feel differently toward your husband if you knew that he prayed for you every day? Would you feel more secure in your relationship and more loved by him? Start praying for him. Pray that he will feel led to intercede for your marriage.

This may seem like an odd prayer to start with. You might be thinking, *Isn't this a waste of time? Why should I put so much effort into praying about my husband's prayers? I want him to help out with the car pool. I need him to be more productive around the house. I want him to learn to communicate better. Shouldn't I be praying for those things more? What's the point of praying for my husband to be a great intercessor?*

I'm glad you asked. Here are five reasons to pray about your husband's prayers:

1. *Prayer will make him love Jesus more deeply.* Men who pray are men who fall in love with Jesus. That's the inevitable and joyous result of time spent in prayer—you learn to love Jesus. If your husband loves Jesus, he's going to be a better husband, father, friend, worker, and Christian. If your husband loves Jesus more deeply, he's going to love you more deeply.

2. *Prayer will make him gentler.* Prayer breaks down a man's pride and gives him perspective on himself. It rounds off his rough edges. Prayer is the incubator of Christlikeness for every Christian. Men who pray are men who learn to rein in their tempers and submit their emotions to Christ. Do you want to have a gentle husband? Pray that he will be a man of prayer.

3. *Prayer will make him more forgiving.* Prayer dispenses forgiveness. Through prayer, men of God confess their sins and find grace and mercy in return. Praying men learn to be forgiven and to forgive. In Luke 7, Jesus told Simon the Pharisee that men who had been forgiven much loved much (see v. 47). Simon, who hadn't yet realized his own need for forgiveness, didn't know how to love another sinner. Praying and confessing men do. As your husband prays and confesses, receiving

God's forgiveness, he'll also learn to extend that forgiveness.

4. *Prayer will help him hate sin.* Prayer and sin are antithetical. They don't coexist well. A heart that neglects prayer naturally drifts toward sin; a praying heart will hate it. Prayer roots in the very soul of a man and exposes what's really there. In a man's quiet moments of prayer and reflection, the Holy Spirit will find his heart soft and pliable. The Spirit can then easily reveal to the praying man if lust, fear, anger, pride, insecurity, jealousy, hatred, doubt, stubbornness, selfishness, bitterness, and resentment are residing in his heart. God launches holy ambushes for a man as he prays. If you want your husband to hate sin, pray for his prayer life.

5. *Prayer will show him where he's going.* Jesus found direction in prayer. He knew when to stay in a village and when to move on. He knew when to invest his time in healing the sick and when to pull away and pour himself into his disciples. Jesus also found the strength to face the cross and bear up under its agony, and he did so through prayer. Praying men will eventually figure out where they're going in life. They'll have a clear sense of direction and purpose and will typically have the spiritual discipline to not stray from it. Praying men are well-led men—they're led by the Holy Spirit. As your husband becomes a man of prayer, he will become better equipped to discern where God is leading him.

Do you have the faith to pray about your husband's prayer life? Are you willing to release your husband to Jesus and give the Holy Spirit time to accomplish his work in your man's life? Praying for your husband to be a mighty man of prayer will change both of you. Start asking God for that today. You have everything to gain and nothing to lose.

Pray Big Prayer Starter
Pray Colossians 4:2 for your husband—
Lord, please help my husband to devote himself to prayer.

Pray that he will be a great leader. Jesus is the ultimate trustworthy leader. He never leads us astray or into a situation he can't handle. He knows how hard to push his followers, and he knows when to slow down and give them time to catch up. Jesus knows how to inspire vision and motivate us to great things.

Pray that your husband will lead like Jesus. Pray that he'll be wise and discerning. Ask God to help him make good decisions and be a trustworthy steward of the leadership mantle that God has given him.

I once talked to a woman whose husband had made so many poor business and career decisions that she started to feel she was being irresponsible to continue following him. She was slowly starting to take over the reins of leadership in her home because, in her eyes, her husband had clearly disqualified himself. She had basically given up on him and wasn't praying for him. While I don't blame her for her skepticism, the reality is that she was not only quietly usurping his authority in the home, she was also doubting that God ultimately would provide for her needs.

Your husband is never going to be a perfect leader, but he can become a better one. Start pinpoint praying that he'll learn to lead as Jesus does. Pray also for yourself—that you'll be patient with him and submissive to him. Pray for grace to give your husband time to respond to the Holy Spirit's leadership in his life. Remember to look to God, not to your man, as your ultimate source of security.

Pray Big Prayer Starter

Pray Matthew 11:28–30 for your husband—
Father, help my husband to lead like Jesus. Make him wise, godly, and easy to follow. As I yield to him, may I be joyful and find rest for my soul.

Pray that he will be a great lover. As you read Ephesians 5:25, it becomes obvious that love is the primary motive of Christ as the husband of the church: "Husbands, love your wives, just as Christ loved the church." Every word Christ speaks, every command he issues, and every action he takes on behalf of his bride is driven by love. He doesn't know how to respond out of greed or selfishness; all Christ knows is white-hot passion for his bride.

Pray that your husband will be the kind of lover that Jesus is. Pray that he will be motivated in his dealings with you by his great love for you. Ask God to give him the same unconditional love for you that Jesus has for his church.

I saw a great example of this kind of love in one of my doctoral professors. He was a retired missionary who taught young, aspiring ministers about prayer and personal disciplines. He was having a very effective ministry on the seminary campus when his wife of several decades was stricken with a terrible degenerative disease.

At first, my professor was able to continue teaching and still provide adequate care for his wife. But after a few years, her condition became so bad that he actually retired from teaching so that he could care for her full time. A few years after that, his bride became so ill and care-dependent that she had to be placed in a nursing home. My professor, not wanting to abandon his bride in her most desperate hour, actually sold their home and moved into the nursing home with her. He was a totally healthy, alert, and functioning man, very capable of still being extremely productive, who felt it was his God-given duty to stay at his wife's side. And he did that for several years until she died.

Few men or women can hold to that level of love and commitment without Christ. I certainly can't. But with Christ, ordinary, sinful men like me are equipped to love their wives with the same kind of passion, fidelity, and tenacity that Jesus shows toward us. Pray that for your husband. Pray that he'll love you like Jesus does.

Pray Big Prayer Starter

Pray Matthew 1:19 for your husband—
*Lord, give my husband a heart like Joseph's.
Make him a righteous man who
always desires to treat me nobly.*

Pray that he will be a great provider. Jesus knows how to meet needs. His love and passion for his bride motivate him to always provide for her needs. He comes by this giving spirit naturally. One of the names for God in the Old Testament is Jehovah-Jireh, the Lord who provides (see Gen. 22:13–14). Jesus became God's ultimate provision for us when he died for our sins. Paul, reflecting on the providing character of God, promised the believers in Philippi that "my God will meet all your needs according to his glorious riches in Christ Jesus" (Phil. 4:19).

Do you want to pray a powerful pinpoint prayer for your husband? Pray that he will take seriously his God-given assignment to provide for his family. This does not mean that your husband has to be the sole or even primary breadwinner in your home. It means that it is his responsibility to make sure his family's needs are met. The Lord Jesus works through various agencies—human and divine—when providing for his church. You and your husband may agree to provide for your family's needs through his or your income, or through a combination of the two. God does not mandate the method.

He does command that your husband take seriously his role as provider and that those under his care are well fed, protected, clothed, and nurtured (see 1 Tim. 5:8).

When Jesus meets the needs of his church, he does not necessarily meet all of her *wants*. Christ frequently says no when what we want exceeds or works against what we need. You need to pray that your husband doesn't feel pressure to work sixty to eighty hours a week to make sure you have a certain comfy lifestyle. Many wives pressure hardworking husbands to work even harder so that they can achieve the next level of status financially. That, quite bluntly, is nowhere in the biblical job description of a providing husband.

Part of what a godly leader needs to provide for his family is spiritual leadership and instruction. That's difficult to do if he is always chasing after the next version of the American dream. Pray that your husband will have the wisdom to know the difference between provision and indulgence.

Several years ago a family from Ohio moved to Austin and started attending our church. The husband had taken a higher-paying job that required him to relocate. The family left behind many longtime friends and a great church. Not long after they started attending our church, I shared a message about what provision meant. I talked about how a man's provision of spiritual leadership and quality time for his family was more important than financial prosperity.

The husband and wife were both greatly convicted by the Holy Spirit. They determined that their move to Austin had been motivated by the wrong things. They concluded that they had given up what really mattered in order to pursue what didn't. As a result of this realization, the husband called up his former employer and asked if he could have his job back. The employer immediately agreed. The family moved back to Ohio and reconnected with their church community. Every member of the family was thrilled with that decision. The last time I talked with them, they were doing quite well. God has repeatedly affirmed their decision to return to Ohio.

Pray that your husband will never feel pressure from you, himself, or anyone else to keep up with the Joneses. Pray that Jesus's standard of provision will be what he aspires to.

Pray Big Prayer Starter

Pray 1 Timothy 5:8 for your husband—
*Lord, help my husband to faithfully
provide for the needs of our family.*

Pray that he will have a servant's heart. As the husband of the church, Jesus modeled a servant's spirit. He taught that he didn't come to be served but to serve others (see Matt. 20:28) and that people in authority should lead through serving (see Mark 10:41–45). The apostle Paul showed us beautifully how Jesus's descent into humanity and humility was motivated by his servant orientation (see Phil. 2:5–9). Even though he is King and Lord of the church, Jesus is also his bride's chief servant.

What a paradox: he who could rightfully flex his muscles and force his way doesn't. He who is entitled to boast and brag chooses not to. He who should be served instead serves. Pray the same for your husband. Pray that he will have the heart of a servant.

A friend of mine recently proposed to his sweetheart. I told you about my own disastrous proposal efforts in an earlier chapter. This guy makes all the rest of us guys look really bad. If there was a reward given for the most profound and biblical marriage proposal ever, I think my friend would be a winner.

As part of his proposal, my friend got down on his knees before his girlfriend and washed her feet. He wanted her to know that he understood his role in their relationship. He wanted her to know that he was in it to serve. Don't get me wrong, this guy is no pushover. He's big and strong and a man's man. He's a leader in the church and in the marketplace. That's why what he did is so profound. He could feel entitled to boast and brag and try to control his girl, but he doesn't. The Holy Spirit has shown him another way to lead. So he washed his girlfriend's feet, and he did so as a metaphor of how he intended to approach their marriage.

Pray that your husband will have a servant's heart. Pray that he'll take his cues from Jesus, not culture, for how he should lead and treat you. Pray that he will be secure enough in his relationship with God to humble himself before you and be a servant leader.

Pray Big Prayer Starter

Ask God to give your man a Philippians 2:3 attitude—*Lord, help my husband to do nothing out of selfish ambition or vain conceit but in humility consider others better than himself.*

Pray the same thing for yourself. Remember that the church, in her passion for and commitment to Christ, lives to serve him every day. As you pray about your husband's servant attitude, pray about yours as well. If you want him to approach you humbly, then approach him humbly. Don't just pray for him to serve you and meet your needs; pray also that you'll joyfully serve him and meet his.

It's Worth the Wait

It's possible that while reading this chapter you may have become frustrated with what your husband *isn't*. You've been reading about all the great things Jesus is, wishing that your husband would become more like him. Don't allow frustration to steal your joy, and don't give up on your man. Philippians 1:6 promises that God isn't done working in either of you. As long as you're living this side of heaven, the Holy Spirit will be working on you both. So keep praying!

There is a promise in Galatians that will help you pray and be patient as God does his great work in your husband. It reads, "For we through the Spirit, by faith, are waiting for the hope of righteousness" (Gal. 5:5 NASB). Paul's emphasis in that verse is on how God's grace, not our own efforts, changes us and makes us holy. In other words, *righteousness is not something you can achieve; it is something you must receive.* There are four prominent nouns in Galatians 5:5—*Spirit, faith, hope,* and *righteousness.* There is only one verb—*waiting.* As God makes us holy, through faith we have to wait and depend on him to do his work in us.

Now apply this verse to your husband. As you pray for him to become more like Christ, this verse tells you exactly what's required for that to happen:

- *The Holy Spirit*—Only he can produce change in your man's life.
- *Faith*—You have to believe God's promise to answer your prayers and to work in your man.
- *Hope*—Your prayers and the promises of God's Word will produce great hope in you for your husband.
- *Righteousness*—Holiness and righteousness are the goal of the Spirit's work in your man's life.
- *Waiting*—Time is required for a real life change to occur in your husband.

I hope you'll talk to the Lord every day about your husband, and I hope you'll do it with the language of Galatians 5:5.

- Tell God that you trust the Holy Spirit to accomplish his great work in your man's life. Submit in prayer to the Spirit's agenda, not your own, for your husband.
- Tell God you believe his Word and that you know he will come through for you and your man.
- Ask God to increase your hope for your husband and your marriage. Pray that your hope of God's work in your man will equip you to remain faithful and obedient to Jesus in the potentially difficult days of change that lie ahead.
- Pray that your husband will hunger and thirst for God's righteousness (see Matt. 5:6).
- Ask God for the strength and grace to wait patiently for the Spirit to complete his work in your husband. Tell God that you will give him all the time necessary to do so.

If your husband isn't yet the Christian that you want him to be or think he needs to be, I want to encourage you to wait for him and not bail out on him. Don't try to manipulate the outcome, and don't give God a deadline. Your husband can change. Be as patient in waiting for him to mature as Christ has been in waiting for you. Don't be judgmental, don't become bitter, and don't start thinking that you deserve better. Remember that you are "married" first and foremost to Jesus. Draw your comfort and strength from him as he works to make your husband a mighty man of God.

I've seen countless examples of God answering the pinpoint prayers of wives. I've seen men who were completely uninterested in the things of God become praying, serving, worshiping, and godly followers of Christ. Behind all of those dramatic changes were the prayers of a faithful, patient woman. Pray for your husband. God *will* answer your prayers.

Pray Big Today

- Pray that your husband will love God's Word and will regularly read the Bible.
- Pray that he will hate sin.
- Pray that he will love to pray and be a man of prayer.
- Pray that your husband will welcome Christian community in his life and be accountable to at least one Christian man.
- Pray that your husband will love to worship.
- Pray that he will understand the significance of fighting for his family spiritually.
- Pray that he will be a mighty warrior of God.

Verses to Pray for Your Husband

- 2 Timothy 1:7: *Lord, please help my husband to not have a spirit of timidity, but give him a spirit of power, love, and self-discipline.*
- 2 Corinthians 10:3–4: *Father, teach my husband to not wage war as the world does. Help him to not fight with weapons of the world. Give him your power, O God, to demolish satanic strongholds in our home and family.*
- Luke 9:23: *Holy God, help my husband to deny himself, take up his cross daily, and follow Jesus.*

105

A Marriage Pinpoint Prayer

Lord God, I pray for my husband. I ask that you make him a mighty man of God. Fill him daily with your Spirit and help him to walk in your paths. I pray that he will be a man of worship and prayer, a man who loves your Word and who hates sin. Please help him to always speak with integrity and honesty. Make him a Christ-follower who is above reproach. I ask that you make him a great leader in our marriage and that you give me the grace to submit to him as I submit to you. I pray this in Jesus's awesome name. Amen.

8

How to Pray
for Your Wife

Picture the scene: a man on his knees, his face toward heaven, his hands open in a palms-up gesture. He is praying. He has been for a while. This is no casual prayer or pray-er. This man means business. He intercedes with great intensity and is totally focused on what he's asking.

He is praying for his bride. He prays for her beauty, her purity, her protection, and her prosperity. He is asking God to grant her favor in all that she does. On and on he goes, seeking God's best for his beautiful bride.

He is the ultimate praying husband. Who is he? The Lord Jesus. In John 17 we find the longest recorded prayer of Jesus in Scripture. On the night of his betrayal and subsequent crucifixion, Jesus spent many of his final moments of freedom praying. Much of his praying consisted of intercessions for his bride, the church.

I find that to be a profound and inspiring truth: in Jesus's final hours, not only did he pray, but he prayed for us, his bride. As a husband, I'm both humbled and challenged by Jesus's example. It makes me want to pray more for my wife. It makes me want to be the kind of intercessor that Jesus was.

Step Up to the Plate

Unfortunately, I've dealt with far too many marriages in which the husband has checked out spiritually. Women are typically more spiritually intuitive than men anyway, and most men seem perfectly happy to let them take the lead. Such spiritual abdication by Christian men is not only sinful and unbiblical, it's also devastating to our marriages, our homes, and our nation. Christian men and women both have biblically assigned roles to play. When either a Christian husband or wife drops their end of the rope, far too much pressure is placed on the other to take up the slack. Specifically, in many cases Christian women are required to play both the role of wife and spiritual leader because the husband is out fishing (figuratively or literally). As a result, they're unable to do either role very well.

Husbands, I'm asking you to step up to the plate. I'm asking you to acknowledge and accept your biblical role as a man and leader. Don't dump your responsibilities on your wife. If you skipped the last chapter, thinking it was just for your wife, go back and read it. Find out what she is praying for you to become, then make a decision to be that kind of man. Be a man who loves Jesus more than anything else. Be a man who has his appetites and attitudes firmly submitted to Jesus's authority. Embrace the role model of the Lord Jesus and become a praying husband. Become your wife's number one intercessor.

Why Should You Pray for Your Wife?

The greatest gift you can give your wife is the gift of prayer. I'm not overstating that. Consistent, biblical, specific praying will not only help and encourage your wife and your relationship with her, it will also change *you*. I've watched prayer deepen and strengthen my relationship with Susie over the years. I know it can do the same for your relationship with your bride.

Here are some biblical reasons for you to become your wife's primary intercessor.

You are called to love her as Jesus does. The apostle Paul's command in Ephesians 5 couldn't be any clearer: "Husbands, love your wives, just as Christ loved the church and gave himself up for her" (Eph. 5:25). In other words, "Husband, love your wife as Jesus loves you; love her enough to die for her." The type of love Paul mentions in that verse is the lofty and noble kind that exists between Jesus and God as members of the Trinity. It is the love described in John 3:16 that led God to give his Son as a sacrifice for sinners. This high and holy love is the unconditional, unwavering covenant love modeled by God in his relationship with the rebellious nation of Israel. And it is the type of love that is impossible for humans to show others without the ongoing work of God's Spirit in their lives.

Left to yourself, you'll never be able to love your wife adequately. The command to love her as Jesus loves you will elude you, despite your best efforts. But praying every day—asking God to equip you with his love and grace for your wife—will go a long way toward helping you fulfill your biblical assignment to love your bride as Jesus loves you. Prayer can give you the humility, patience, self-control, and vision to rise to the occasion and serve your wife.

I learned this firsthand several years ago. Susie and I were going through a bumpy time in our marriage. I was shedding years of emotional and relational baggage, and my healing process had created a prolonged season of tension in our marriage. Whenever I grew impatient with Susie and with what I perceived to be her prickly attitude toward me, I would call my accountability partner, Rick, to gripe about what a victim I was. He would listen to me for about ten seconds and then always ask the same question that inevitably led to a conversation I didn't want to have. The scenario would typically go something like this:

> **Rick:** Okay, Will, so you're put out with how Susie is acting.
>
> **Me:** Yep. Pretty much.
>
> **Rick:** And you want things to change.
>
> **Me:** Yep.
>
> **Rick:** I think I can help. Let me ask you a question: how far did Jesus go to serve you?
>
> **Me:** Excuse me?
>
> **Rick:** How far did Jesus go to serve you?
>
> **Me:** I don't understand the question.
>
> **Rick:** Come on, Will, it's not that hard. How far did Jesus go to serve you? What did he do?
>
> **Me:** That's not fair; that's not the same thing.
>
> **Rick:** Yes, it is. How far did he go?
>
> **Me:** He died.
>
> **Rick:** What? I couldn't hear you.
>
> **Me:** *He died!*
>
> **Rick:** That's right; he died for your sorry butt. And since he's your Lord and Master and your role model for how to act in marriage, how far are you supposed to go to serve Susie?
>
> **Me:** I really don't like you.

Rick: Answer the question. How far?

Me: I'm supposed to die for her.

Rick: That's right! You're supposed to die for her. And now, Will, I have a final question: are you dead yet?

Me: No.

Rick: Right again! No, Will, you're not dead. You're complaining and calling to tell me how bad you've got it. And since you're obviously not dead, shut up and go back to serving Susie. Call me when you're dead.

I always hated those conversations. But Rick was right, and I would inevitably humble myself before God and Susie and go back to praying for her. In my prayers, God would break me, teach me, and give me the equipping I needed to love Susie the way he wanted me to. In the end, God did a major work in us both.

You need to pray for your wife simply because God's call on your life requires it. You won't be able to fulfill your biblical role without prayer.

Pray Big Prayer Starter

Pray for your own prayer life. Ask God to make you a mighty intercessor. Pray that he'll lead and equip you to pray effectively for your bride.

You are called to serve her as Jesus does. One of the primary ways that Jesus serves us is through prayer. We've already seen that he spent much of his final night on earth praying for his bride, the church. Did you know that his intercessions didn't stop when he went to heaven? Hebrews 7:25 tells us that Jesus is still praying for us: "He is able to save completely those who come to God through him, because he always lives to intercede for them."

111

If Jesus always lives to intercede for his bride, and if we're supposed to serve our wives as Jesus serves us, then it makes sense that we should develop a lifetime habit of praying for our spouses. The phrase "I promise to love, honor, cherish, and pray for you, until death alone do us part" probably should be a part of every man's marriage vows.

Gary and Jackie Sinclair are a delightful couple who recently moved to Austin from the Midwest so Gary could serve on our church staff. A few years before the move, doctors discovered a cancerous tumor in Jackie's colon. Instantly, Jackie and Gary's "normal" was consumed with months of tests, chemotherapy, radiation, checkups, doctor visits, medications, surgeries, and even some discouraging setbacks.

The Sinclairs had been married for nearly thirty years and had relied on prayer to guide them through many important decisions and seasons of life. But in this new crisis, Gary felt called to take his prayers for his wife to an entirely new level. After Jackie's diagnosis, he made a new commitment to her: he was going to pray over her every night for the next year, no matter what. Gary knew that God could do whatever he wanted with Jackie. He could heal her or take her home to heaven. But Gary determined that whatever the result, it would be against the backdrop of his pouring out his heart for his wife every night in prayer.

Gary kept his promise to Jackie. There were weeks when his praying appeared to have little impact, but he kept on. There were nights when Jackie was so weakened from her treatments that she didn't know he was praying over her, but he prayed anyway.

God honored Gary's prayers. Today Jackie is doing well, and there doesn't appear to be any sign of cancer in her body. And while neither of them can explain all the implications of those months of prayer, they know that God brought them closer together through those prayers. Their spiritual intimacy grew as Gary prayed daily over his wife. Today their prayer practice continues, not as ritual or requirement but out of a love for God and each other that deepened as they prayed their way through the valley of the shadow of death.

Do you want to serve your wife? Are you ready to be the kind of husband that Jesus is to his bride? Then start praying.

Pray Big Prayer Starter

Ask God to make you the type of husband Jesus is. Ask him to help you live to intercede for your wife. Pray for wisdom and insight to intercede for her according to God's Word.

You are called to lead her as Jesus does. In Ephesians 5:22, the apostle Paul gave women one of the most misunderstood commands in the Bible: "Wives, submit to your husbands as to the Lord." I'm quite sure that the Holy Spirit never intended for all the controversy to develop around this simple command, but centuries of abuse and misapplication by the church have made the topic of submission a negative one for many women. It doesn't have to be. Note that the command is for your wife to submit to you as she would to the Lord. She has to discern through prayer and reading God's Word what her submission to you looks like in practical terms. You need to imitate Jesus to the degree that her submission to you will be as joyful and easy as it is to Christ.

To fulfill your biblical duty as a husband, you need to be the kind of leader that Jesus is. How does Jesus lead? He leads gently, patiently, wisely, and steadily. It is a joy for his followers to submit to him because he is such a great leader. Know also that Jesus's leadership is never forced. Every person who follows him *chooses* to. To lead like Jesus does, you need to be the kind of leader that your wife will gladly follow. Be patient, kind, steady, and trustworthy in your leadership. Make it easy for her to follow you.

How do you become that kind of leader? Through prayer.

Pray Big Prayer Starter

Pray Matthew 20:25–28 for your leadership in your home—*Lord, help me to not "lord it over" or be bossy with my wife. Instead, help me to become her servant. Help me, like you, to seek to serve and not to be served.*

Pinpoint Prayers to Pray for Your Wife

In January of 2007, Chicago schoolteacher Colleen Pavelka chose to have the birth of her second child induced a few days early so her husband, Mark, a rabid Chicago Bears fan, could attend the Bears' NFC Championship Game against the New Orleans Saints. Now I know that many of you guys reading this are silently thinking, *What a woman!* and praying that your own wife might be equally sold out to your recreational passions. May I suggest, fellow sports fans, that we aim higher in our prayers for our wives? With all due respect to Mark Pavelka and the All-American Colleen, let's pray for more than just a wife who yields to our every desire. Let's pray biblical, powerful, focused prayers for the woman God has blessed us with.

Below are several pinpoint prayers for you to pray for your wife. They're taken directly from the pages of Scripture. These are a few of the verses I pray regularly for Susie. These are only to help get you started. I know that as you read and pray through the Bible, God will give you specific promises you can pray for your wife.

Pray that she will be a woman of character. Proverbs 31:10 observes, "A wife of noble character who can find? She is worth far more than rubies." The term "noble character" means "strong," "substantive," "capable," or "excellent." It's used to describe great armies and great riches. It refers to an unbending inner strength. In this description, the biblical writer sees a woman with an unshakable moral reputation. He sees a woman of impeccable personal integrity. A wife of such character is more valuable to her husband than a collection of rubies.

There is significant cultural pressure on women these days to *be* a character rather than to *have* character. The popular bumper sticker WELL-BEHAVED WOMEN RARELY MAKE HISTORY sums up the new cultural call for women to make headlines, regardless of how or for what. And make headlines they do. We are bombarded with story after story of the new breed of woman who throws caution to the wind and lives as her appetites dictate.

Contrast this new cultural norm with the biblical character Mary, the mother of Jesus. A mere teen when given perhaps the toughest assignment in history, Mary stayed faithful to herself, her husband, and her God. She neither doubted God nor complained when asked to walk a path that would thrust her into a difficult spotlight, not just for the rest of her life, but throughout history. Her character was strong; she was noble indeed.

Pray that God will give your wife a character like Mary's. Ask God to make her strong and steady in the face of the cultural onslaught to become something less than noble. Pray that she won't yield to the gravitational pull of cultural decline.

Pray Big Prayer Starter

Pray 1 Timothy 3:11 for your wife. Ask God to help her be worthy of respect, not a malicious talker but temperate and trustworthy in everything.

Pray that she will delight in God. Psalm 37:4 declares, "Delight yourself in the LORD and he will give you the desires of your heart." It's easy for Christ-following women to get distracted today. The apostle Paul warned the believers in Corinth about being pulled away from their sincere and pure devotion to Christ (see 2 Cor. 11:1–3). We need to pray that our spouses will heed the same warning.

Our wives have so many things competing for their attention. Consider all the media messages they receive on a daily basis: be skinny, be trendy, be cute, do something about those wrinkles around your eyes, your buns are too big, your breasts are too small, get a personal trainer and train for a triathlon, get nicer shoes, try this new makeup, get invited to the club, be pretty, change your hair, be a mom, make at least $100,000 a year, volunteer, update your wardrobe, update your house, keep your husband happy. With all that background noise, it is hard to imagine how any Christian woman could stay focused on Christ.

As a loving husband, you need to pray against those voices that would steal your wife's spiritual passion and distract her from her first love, Jesus. Pray that she'll find her worth in God, not in what the world offers.

Consider another Mary in the Bible, the sister of Martha and Lazarus. When Jesus showed up at their house, Mary sat down at his feet and listened to him teach. Even with Martha complaining that she was neglecting her housework, Mary stayed focused on Jesus. She didn't let others' expectations of her dictate who she should be. Jesus affirmed her for making the right choice (see Luke 10:38–42).

Did you see the rest of the promise in Psalm 37:4? "He will give you the desires of your heart." Those who delight themselves in God will have their hearts fulfilled by him. As your wife's values shift from pleasing others to pleasing God, she'll find her heart is more contented. Pray Psalm

37:4 for your wife. Ask God to help her delight in him. Pray that as she does, her heart will be more and more satisfied.

Pray Big Prayer Starter

Pray Matthew 6:33 for your wife—
Father, teach my wife to seek first your kingdom and your righteousness. As she does, please give her everything she needs.

Pray that she will pursue inner beauty. Ask God to help her overcome the pressure to look a certain way or be attractive by culture's standards. Andrée Seu offers insight into the pressure that women face to look a certain way: "Summer is upon us, and men have no idea what women in this far-flung land go through. The anxiety starts building in March . . . when there will be no more disguising another year's ravages of gravity and the culinary lapses of winter. . . . Naomi Wolf, in her bombshell of a book, *The Beauty Myth*, informed us that '30,000 women told researchers that they would rather lose ten to fifteen pounds than achieve any other goal.'"[1]

Proverbs 31:30 observes, "Charm is deceptive, and beauty is fleeting; but a woman who fears the LORD is to be praised." Pray that your bride will know how deceptive and fleeting physical beauty really is. Pray that she'll fear God and seek him with all her heart. Ask God to protect her from the cultural lie that says looking good is the bottom line.

Pray Big Prayer Starter

Pray Psalm 139:14 for your wife.
Pray that she will know that she is
fearfully and wonderfully made.

Pray that she will know her life's mission. Many women spend their entire lives seeking purpose. Some cultural and religious settings still communicate that women are second-tier citizens. Some women feel that they must live forever in the shadow of the men around them. Many never feel the freedom to pursue their own ministry or life's mission from God.

Susie has wrestled with this very issue. For years she lived in my shadow as the supportive pastor's wife. She put up with my long hours and encouraged me while I got my master's and doctoral degrees, then followed me while I planted two churches and served at a third.

But during that time, Susie couldn't shake the feeling that there was still more for her. She had hopes and dreams of her own ministry that she believed were God-given. Susie and I never stopped praying for God to fulfill those dreams. He was faithful. Today Susie is an accomplished communicator for Christ. She's a published writer and speaks all over the nation, helping women deepen their relationships with God.

Does your wife have a dream? Has she set aside her own hopes and visions so that she might serve yours? Pray for your wife. Ask God to give her a clear life mission.

Think about Esther. It wasn't for her own benefit that she became queen of a nation. God used her strategic placement to save the Jewish nation from extermination. Her "for such a time as this" realization gave her a purpose far beyond her own life. God showed her how, through her obedience, she could minister to countless others (see Esther 4:13–14).

Pray that God will give your wife a "for such a time as this" vision. Ask him to grant her a clear purpose and mission for her life. Pray that she will understand why God gave her the gifts, skills, talents, and experiences she has. Pray that she will be able to embrace and enjoy God's unique calling on her life.

Pray Big Prayer Starter

Pray that you will be supportive and encouraging of your wife's vision. Ask God to free you from any jealousy, insecurity, or selfishness that would keep you from fully blessing her life's mission.

Pray that she will be holy. In Ephesians 5, Paul elaborates on why Jesus died for his bride, the church: "to make her holy, cleansing her by the washing with water through the word, and to present her to himself as a radiant church, without stain or wrinkle or any other blemish, but holy and blameless" (vv. 26–27). Since Jesus prayed for his bride to be holy, we should pray the same for ours.

When a person becomes a Christian, God begins the process of making him or her holy. That process is called *sanctification.* God uses pain, his Word, prayer, worship, tests, and the daily work of his Spirit to recreate the image of Christ in every one of us. The more we allow Jesus to rule and reign in our lives, the holier we will be. Pray for your wife's sanctification process. Pray that God will make her holy.

Now, you may be thinking, *Why should I pray for her to be holy? I'm never going to see the effects of that prayer. Shouldn't I pray for something more tangible?* Actually, whenever you or your spouse grows in holiness, it can have a profound and positive impact on your marriage:

- Holy people hate sin—they're less likely to engage in risky or selfish behaviors.
- Holy people serve—they're quick to submit in love and to place others' needs before their own.
- Holy people give—they love to be generous with their time and resources.

119

- Holy people are wise and discerning—they know how to apply God's teachings to very specific situations in life.
- Holy people forgive—they obey Jesus's command to not hold grudges against anyone.
- Holy people love—they readily extend to others the unconditional love and favor that God has shown them.

Can you see how your wife's increasing holiness can help your marriage? But before you start praying for her holiness so you'll benefit, remember that your role model as a Christian husband is Jesus. Jesus leads and sets the example for his bride. So to whatever degree your wife loves, serves, forgives, gives to, and submits to you, you have to do even more for her! Perhaps you should pray for holiness for *both* of you.

When you pray for your wife to be holy, you're praying in complete agreement with the Holy Spirit. He prays and works for the holiness of every Christ-follower. You couldn't pray a more potent or biblical pinpoint prayer for your wife. So as you pray for her holiness, know that God will answer it and will honor your marriage in the process.

Pray Big Today

- Pray for your role as a Christian husband. Memorize Ephesians 5:25 and think about how Jesus loves and serves you. Pray that you will treat your wife exactly as Jesus treats you. Pray that your wife will find it easy and a joy to submit to you.
- Pray to be a gentle leader. Ask God to help you to not take advantage of the leadership role he has given you

in your home. Pray that you'll be a humble and selfless leader.

- Pray for peace in your home. Ask God to give you and your wife maturity in your disagreements. Pray that the peace and unity of Jesus will be reflected in your marriage.
- Pray for your wife's faith. Ask God to help her believe his Word and trust in his promises. Pray that she won't be inclined to worry.
- Pray for your wife's spiritual disciplines. Ask God to help her love to pray, worship, and read the Bible.
- Pray that your wife will hate sin. Ask God to convict her of sin and to make her quick to repent.
- Pray that your wife will practice instant obedience. Pray that she won't try to negotiate or arm wrestle with God but will have the faith to immediately do whatever he asks.

Verses to Pray for Your Wife

- Ephesians 5:26–27: *Lord, please make my wife holy. Cleanse her through your Word, and present her to yourself as a radiant bride, without stain or wrinkle or any other blemish, but as holy and blameless.*
- Psalm 37:4: *Holy God, please help my wife to delight in you, and give her the desires of her heart.*
- 1 Peter 3:3–4: *Lord, let my wife's beauty come not from outward adornment such as braided hair, jewelry, and fine clothes. Instead, let it come from her inner self—the unfading beauty of a gentle and quiet spirit, which is of great worth in your sight.*

121

A Marriage Pinpoint Prayer

Holy Father, I pray for my sweet wife. Thank you for giving her to me. Help me to see her as the gift that she is. Forgive me for the times I judge her or take her for granted. I pray for her as you prayed for your bride: make her holy. I pray that she will be presented to you holy and without blemish or stain. Complete your great work of sanctification in her life. And, Lord, help me to be a worthy leader for her. Give me the kind of passion, love, and unconditional favor for my bride that you have for yours. I pray this in Jesus's holy name. Amen.

9

How to Pray for Your Unbelieving Spouse

My first clear memory of Eddy Siroin is at my dinner table. I had seen him around the church with his family. I knew that he was a serious Green Bay Packers fan with a life-size cutout of the Packers' legendary quarterback, Brett Favre, in his living room. But as Eddy talked quietly at dinner with a few other couples from our church, I didn't expect what I heard. This kind and quiet man had a deep-seated anger toward God. His language quickly changed from friendly to hostile when I asked him how he felt about spiritual things. Eddy made it very clear that he was in control of his own life. The only reason he went to church was to support his wife and kids. He had no use for God and didn't expect that to change. As far as Eddy was concerned, he and God were just fine *not* relating to each other.

Eddy's wife, Lynn, on the other hand, had grown up in a believing home. Faith came naturally to her. She longed for a marriage relationship that reflected faith in Christ, but she knew she couldn't push Eddy. Lynn knew that her hope for her husband's salvation and a Christian marriage was in her prayers for Eddy, not her preaching to him. And pray she did. Lynn became a regular intercessor for Eddy. She started praying Bible verses for him and tried to model a loving, obedient form of Christianity. She left the rest up to God.

I wonder if you have a similar story. Can you relate to the tension of wanting and needing to evangelize your spouse? The combination of trying to live with and witness to the same person can be extremely explosive. It can also be very frustrating.

This chapter is about hope. I want to increase your confidence in the biblical reality that God wants to save your spiritually lost spouse, and I want to show you what your role is and isn't in the process. Most of all, I want to equip you to pray powerful pinpoint prayers for your unbelieving husband or wife.

The Temptations of the Spiritually Mismatched Christian

Before we talk about specific prayers you can pray for your unbelieving mate, let's talk about the temptations a Christian faces when married to a non-Christian. See if you've fallen prey to any of these common ones:

- *Preaching.* By far the most common, this temptation turns the believing husband or wife into a sort of Billy Graham. A husband might constantly tell his spouse what she's missing, or a wife might preach on and on about how her spouse is messing up their marriage by not following Christ. More subtle "preachers" leave open Bibles around the house, place Christian books or periodicals in the bathroom reading basket, and constantly bombard their spouse with a never-ending stream of Christian music.

- *Pouting.* Pouters sulk, mope, and gripe about the sad state of their spiritual union. They take on a victim mentality and are absolutely no fun to be married to. They typically end up depressing both themselves and their spouse.

- *Protesting.* Protestors are more aggressive than pouters. Far from feeling like victims, they believe they're entitled to something better. They think their spouse owes it to them to become a Christian. In order to accomplish their desired purpose, they go on a marriage strike. The thinking of the protestor goes something like this: *If my spouse isn't willing to step up and follow Christ to help our marriage, then I don't have to step up either. Why should I be the only giver in this relationship? I'm done serving in this marriage.* And with that mind-set, the believing spouse stops investing in the marriage and begins to neglect his or her assigned duties as a husband or wife.

- *Punishing.* Punishers are protestors on steroids. They don't simply stop contributing to the marriage; they take the battle to their mate, seeing them as marriage enemy number one. Punishers try to make things as miserable as possible for their wayward spouse, hoping to somehow torture their spouse into following Jesus through their own bad and unloving behavior. Punishers often end up acting more un-Christian than their unbelieving spouses.

• *Punting.* To punt on a relationship is to decide that it's no longer worth the effort. The frustrated spouse simply decides to quit trying, much like a struggling football offense might choose to punt the ball away to the other team. This temptation is the most disheartening, as believing spouses end up leaving their mate, often without biblical justification. As a pastor, I've seen the tragic circumstances in which divorce is permissible and even advisable biblically, but more frequently I see believing spouses punt their marriage relationship simply because they are tired of the struggle. When believers lose hope for their spouse's salvation and walk out of a marriage, God's kingdom work is thwarted. God never gives up on unbelievers; neither should we.

I'm sure I don't have to tell you that the temptations listed above aren't good options for you. If you're married to an unbeliever, you're still called to model the love and faithfulness of Christ to him or her. Aren't you glad that God didn't treat us in our unbelief the way we sometimes treat our unbelieving mates? You made a covenant with God to love your spouse for better or for worse. Give your spiritually seeking mate the time and freedom, which God gave you, to work out his or her beliefs. Don't rush, don't push, and don't preach.

So what's a husband or wife to do when married to an unbeliever? Go get a pen and write it in the blank below. I think you already know the word.

P_____!

Prayers That Set Captives Free

It's time to get to work. Let's be done with griping about, preaching to, and battling with our unbelieving spouses, and let's get to the God-assigned business of interceding for them. Here are some powerful pinpoint prayers you can pray for your spiritually resistant mate.

Pray for the wind of God's Spirit to blow into your husband's soul. Ezekiel 37 gives us a vivid picture of what God wants to do in the lives of those who don't know him. In a vision, the prophet Ezekiel sees a valley full of dry, dusty bones, which represent the exiled nation of Israel. After showing Ezekiel what he wanted to do, God commanded Ezekiel to pray for a miracle: "Then he said to me, 'Prophesy to the breath; prophesy, son of man, and say to it, "This is what the Sovereign Lord says: Come from the four winds, O breath, and breathe into these slain, that they may live."' So I prophesied as he commanded me, and breath entered them; they came to life and stood up on their feet—a vast army" (Ezek. 37:9–10).

Your unbelieving husband (or wife) is exactly like that valley of dry bones. He needs a miracle if he is to find salvation. He cannot fix what is broken. He needs an act of grace. In other words, he needs the wind of God to blow life into his soul. Pray that for him. Let me give you an example of some of God's powerful wind work.

Several years ago I had been praying that a certain man would attend a weeklong Christian camp with me. That was a big, hairy, audacious prayer, because the man was a very hostile unbeliever. I felt that if this guy could get out of his environment and into a safe Christian setting for a few days, God would speak to him. But the more I prayed, the more the man refused to attend.

As I was leaving town on my way to the camp, I felt moved to stop by the guy's house for one final invite. It was early June, and a rare summer cold front was blowing through our town. The weather was rapidly deteriorating. The man and I stood in his front yard while I listed why I wanted him to attend the camp. At some point in the conversation, I noticed that as I was speaking, the gusts of wind that were on the leading edge of the cold front increased. It seemed like every time I spoke, there would be another gust. I took a chance and told the guy that the wind was God's Spirit telling him to go to camp. I told him that the more he resisted, the harder the wind was going to blow.

What happened next still astounds me. God honored my faith and turned up the volume on the wind. It started *howling* all around us. The more we talked, the more it blew. And the more it blew, the more I told the guy that God was speaking to him. Within just a few minutes, we had to shout to hear each other over the wind. Finally, after about twenty minutes of wind-driven negotiations, the guy placed his hand on my shoulder and shouted, "Tell him to stop! I'll go." And he became a believer at camp.

Do you want the wind of God to blow life into your husband's dead soul? Speak to the wind of God's Spirit as Ezekiel did. Ask God to blow his mighty Spirit into your husband's life with great force and fury until your mate believes.

Pray Big Prayer Starter

Pray Ezekiel 37:9 for your unbelieving spouse—
*Come, O wind of God, and blow your
life into my husband's soul.*

Pray that the Holy Spirit will convict your wife. In the New Testament, we are given a unique look at the work of the Holy Spirit in the life of an unbeliever. Jesus taught us that the Spirit has a very specific job description when it comes to dealing with the spiritually lost. "When he comes, he will convict the world of guilt in regard to sin and righteousness and judgment" (John 16:8). Jesus promised that his Spirit would actively pursue and convict those whose hearts were cold toward him.

Remember that conviction is a good thing. You want the Holy Spirit to convict your wayward wife (or husband). The Spirit's conviction shows her that she is missing something. He speaks to her about Jesus, about her need for righteousness, and about the coming judgment for all who don't believe. Pray that she will be convicted by God's Spirit.

A word of warning: convicted spouses are grumpy spouses. A woman under the conviction of God will not be a happy camper. As the Holy Spirit creates the appropriate dissonance in the life of an unbeliever, she will typically become more irritable. Expect that, and don't be surprised if things get a little bumpy as the Spirit does his holy work. It's a sign that God is at work in your mate's life.

Pray Big Prayer Starter

Pray for God's Spirit to create chaos in the life of your unbelieving spouse. Ask him to take away everything that she looks to for comfort and personal value. Ask the Spirit to show your spouse her need for Jesus.

Pray that your husband's mind will be enlightened to the truth of Jesus. There is a critical text in 2 Corinthians that gives us helpful insight into the plight of unbelievers. According to Paul, unbelievers are spiritually blind: "Even if our gospel is veiled, it is veiled to those who are perishing. The god of this age has blinded the minds of unbelievers, so that they cannot see the light of the gospel of the glory of Christ, who is the image of God" (4:3–4). Satan, the archenemy of Christ, has blinded the minds of all humans to the truth of Christ. Did you note what Satan blinded? Their *minds.*

People frequently reject Christ because they don't think the Christian message makes sense. They have trouble coming to terms with Christ on a rational level.

It's not irrational to believe in Christ. The Bible repeatedly teaches that belief in God and Christ are where true wisdom and knowledge begin. Faith and reason are not mutually exclusive. If your unbelieving husband is to know Christ, then he's going to have to yield his mind to Jesus.

Pray against the blindness that Satan has inflicted on your husband (or wife). Pray that he will see the rationale behind believing. Ask God to expose the lies that have misled him and kept him from faith. Pray that he will be able to see the truth of Jesus.

Pray Big Prayer Starter

Pray 2 Corinthians 4:4 for your mate—*Lord, please remove the blinders from my husband's mind. Help him to see the true light of the gospel of Christ.*

Pray that you will be a positive influence on your wife. There is a salt-and-light factor that can take place in a marriage between a believer and an unbeliever (see Matt. 5:13–16). Being salt or light is not a justifiable reason to marry an unbeliever, but if you are already married to one, pray that God will use his holy presence in you as a sanctifying factor for your wife.

In 1 Corinthians 7, Paul offers an interesting comment on how an unbelieving spouse can be influenced by his or her believing partner: "For the Christian wife brings holiness to her marriage, and the Christian husband brings holiness to his marriage" (v. 14 NLT). Countless gallons of ink have been spilled over the centuries by scholars trying to decipher what exactly Paul meant by these words. For our purposes, let's agree that he was at least saying God can use the holiness of a Christian spouse to seriously impact

130

and sway the heart of an unbeliever. The text is *not* saying that it's your job to save your lost mate. That's God's job. But it *is* your job to be a holy example of God's grace to your mate. As Christians, we need to be shining examples of God's mercy to the lost people around us, especially to our unbelieving spouses.

Peter gives specific instructions to women married to unbelieving men: "Wives, in the same way be submissive to your husbands so that, if any of them do not believe the word, they may be won over without words by the behavior of their wives, when they see the purity and reverence of your lives" (1 Peter 3:1–2). He told them that the biggest impact they could have on their husbands would come through their lives, not their words. If you're married to an unbeliever, remember that truth. It will be your godly and humble submission to Christ that will get his attention, not your persuasive arguments.

Pray Big Prayer Starter

Ask God to make you a holy presence in your home. Pray that your godliness, humility, and joy will have a profound effect on your wife. Pray that your Christian walk will be a help, not a hindrance, to her finding Christ.

Pray that God will surround your husband with his people. You are probably not the person who is going to win your spouse to Christ. You will clearly play a role, as your obedience and godliness impact him, but it will probably be others who carry the load in helping your mate see the truth of Jesus. Pray for those people. Pray that God will surround your spouse with strong and mature Christ-followers.

There's a man in our church who claims to be an agnostic. He is also a gifted musician. His wife, a believer, has done a great job of loving her husband, not preaching to him, and introducing him to other Christians in our church. He joined one of our music teams and participates regularly in our services. He's there for the rehearsals, devotions, and prayers for our events. He hears us rebuke Satan and pray for God's mercy and favor. He has developed several close friendships on the team.

The man is not a believer yet, but he's on his way. He would tell anyone who asks that church has become a major part of his life. He's more committed to church than some of our believers! I firmly believe that someday soon I'll stand in the water with him at his baptism. His wife's godly example, her faithful prayers, and the impact of many other Christians are helping this man overcome his spiritual skepticism.

Pray Big Prayer Starter

Ask God for three Christian friends for your spouse. Pray that he will confide in them, learn from them, and be influenced positively by them. Start praying now for that day when you will all celebrate together at your spouse's baptism.

A Traveling Evangelist

Do you want to know what happened with Eddy and Lynn Siroin, the couple I introduced you to at the beginning of this chapter? Did God answer Lynn's prayers for Eddy?

Lynn decided to be baptized as an act of obedience to Christ. She had been baptized as an infant but not as a Christ-follower. In September of 2003, she was baptized in her backyard pool as a statement of her faith in Christ. Eddy was among those who watched her from the poolside that day. Lynn's obedience started a domino effect of blessing in her and Eddy's lives. By early 2004, Eddy was ready to follow Christ as well. Lynn's prayers and consistent obedience helped create an environment for the Holy Spirit to work in her husband's heart. In March of 2004, Eddy was baptized in his backyard pool, where his wife had been baptized just six months before. God changed his heart, and he used the prayers of a faithful spouse to do so.

Today Eddy and Lynn homeschool their two kids and travel the country, promoting their family RV business. As part of a growing distribution list that Eddy has, I get an email from him every day. He not only tells us where in the United States the Siroin family is that day, but he also sends along a verse of Scripture. He's like a traveling Internet evangelist. Not bad for a Wisconsin cheese-head who wanted nothing to do with God.

Prayer works.

Pray Big Today

- Pray that your spouse will have an unmistakable encounter with the Holy Spirit. Pray for a holy ambush.
- Ask God to show your spouse his need for forgiveness. Pray that he'll be aware of and convicted about his sin.
- Pray for humility for your spouse. Pray that she'll humble herself before God.
- Pray for yourself. Ask God to make you patient, loving, and noncondemning as your spouse wrestles with his faith.
- Pray that you'll be a godly and above-reproach example of the Christian faith.
- Pray every day for your spouse's salvation. Thank Jesus for dying for her and ask him to set her free.

Verses to Pray for You and Your Unbelieving Spouse

- Isaiah 49:25: *Father, you promised that captives would be taken from warriors and plunder retrieved from the fierce. I name my husband as a captive before you and ask you to set him free. Fight the enemy that fights against his salvation and please save him.*
- Luke 4:18–19: *Lord Jesus, you said that God's Spirit anointed you to preach good news to the poor, to proclaim freedom to prisoners and recovery of sight to the blind, to release the oppressed, and to proclaim the year of God's favor. Jesus, please fulfill these purposes in my wife's life. Please proclaim your salvation to her.*
- Matthew 5:13–14: *Lord Jesus, please help me to be a preserving and purifying factor, like salt, in my marriage. Help me to be a light that shines brightly for Jesus's glory in my home.*

A Marriage Pinpoint Prayer

Holy God, I pray for my husband. I ask you to open his eyes and help him to see the truth of your Word. Please free him from the tyranny of Satan that currently rules and reigns in his life. I know he is a captive, so I ask you to set him free. I pray that you will humble me and equip me to love and serve him without judging or preaching to him. Let my life be an example of your love and mercy to him. I ask you to do whatever is necessary in and through me to win him. I submit my life to you fully as a sacrifice. Please take it and use it to bring about my husband's salvation. I pray this in Jesus's name. Amen.

10

PRAYING FOR PROTECTION

Not long ago, I pulled into a local McDonald's to pick up two cups of their fantastic coffee. My wife and I have a significant McDonald's coffee habit, and every morning before dawn I'm there at the drive-through acquiring our daily fix. On this day, as I headed for the drive-through lane, I noticed a woman smiling at me from inside the store. At first it didn't seem odd, but as I drove past the window, she kept looking at me.

My first thought was, *How nice; that woman is giving me a friendly morning smile.* But the longer she stared, the more awkward I felt. She held eye contact with me for several seconds, and I was really starting to grow uncomfortable. My thoughts moved to, *That woman is flirting with me.* She was attractive, she was smiling at me, and she was making no attempt to be subtle or redirect her gaze. I was just about to call my accountability partner when I made an unsettling discovery: the woman was a poster. Hanging in the window of McDonald's was a life-size picture of a lovely woman greeting morning coffee buyers with a friendly smile. I had somehow gotten the impression that she was not only real but that she was flirting with me. Okay, so I'm not the sharpest tool in the shed. I'll just blame it on the poor predawn light and my precoffee condition.

Sin Is Crouching at the Door

Temptation is everywhere. Real temptation. The stuff we face every day is a lot more serious than my poster-in-the-window mistake. You don't have to look very far to find multiple opportunities to foul up your marriage. Co-workers, business trips, flirtatious neighbors, and even overly friendly church members give ample opportunity for us to become enmeshed in inappropriate relationships. Added to that is the never-ending stream of television shows and movies that glorify sex and discredit marriage, as well as Internet pornography that offers exposure to just about any type of sexual deviance and expression from the privacy of your own computer.

But that's not all. Temptation these days can be much more sophisticated. Overpacked schedules, years of pent-up anger and frustration, emotional immaturity and dysfunction, dependence on children, or unhealthy spousal behavior can produce a buffet of areas for Satan to choose from when seeking to derail our marriages.

In the midst of all these opportunities for marriage failure, here's a great prayer for marriage protection: "And lead us not into temptation, but deliver us from the evil one" (Matt. 6:13). This is taken right from the Lord's Prayer. In one sweeping statement, Jesus gives us a powerful weapon against Satan's onslaught. Divided into halves, this prayer becomes two proactive petitions you can add to your marriage prayer arsenal.

Lord, help us to flee temptation. Pray for discernment to recognize temptation before it comes and then to run like crazy whenever you recognize it. Too often we like to flirt with temptation. We want to get close enough to feel the rush of the pleasurable side of sin, but not close enough to get burned. Concerning the allure of an adulterous woman, Solomon warned, "Keep to a path far from her, do not go near the door of her house" (Prov. 5:8). In other words, run away! Don't see how close you can get to the temptation without crossing the line. Just run away.

Pray that you and your spouse will see temptation for what it is. Remember what Jesus said about Satan in John 10:10—he comes to kill, steal, and destroy. Don't give him the chance. Pray that you both will run away when temptation calls.

Lord, protect us from Satan. Perhaps you've heard this statement: God loves you and has a wonderful plan for your life. Well, the reverse is true of Satan: he hates you and has a terrible plan for your life, including your marriage. Every Christ-following couple intent on having a God-honoring marriage needs to be aware that Satan is determined to attack their relationship. If he can, he will destroy it. Few things honor God more than a Christ-centered marriage; few things attract the ire of Satan more.

Don't be intimidated by Satan. God has given you all the equipping you need to keep him at bay. But don't be naive either. Pray every day for God's protection and covering from Satan's ploys on your marriage.

Pray Big Prayer Starter

Pray the Lord's Prayer regularly for your marriage. Ask God to build his kingdom and do his will in your marriage. Ask him to provide for the needs of your marriage, to forgive your sins, to help you to be forgiving toward your spouse, and to protect your marriage from evil.

Praying a Hedge around Your Marriage

Let's get to the business of praying for protection for the most common marriage foes. The prophet Hosea, who lived in the eighth century BC, prayed that God would place a hedge of thorns around his wife, Gomer, to keep her in and temptation out (see Hos. 2:6). Let's pray the same prayer for our marriages. Below are some of the most common threats to marriage I see every day in the lives of Christian couples, and biblical ways to pray against them.

Bitterness and unforgiveness. "I don't love her anymore. That's the bottom line. I just don't love her." Things weren't going well in this counseling session. The man who sat before me was a member of the church I lead, but more than that, he was becoming a friend. I had picked up on the subtle signs that his marriage might be sailing through rough seas, so I'd asked if we could meet to talk about things. Fortunately, he agreed to, but that's where the good news stopped.

This guy was a mess. Years of unresolved conflict and unforgiveness had turned his insides into emotional mush. He was severely wounded and didn't even know it. He was also angry—angry at God, at his parents, at the church, and, most of all, at his wife. No wonder his marriage was in trouble.

Has the bug of bitterness infected your marriage? Once it takes root, it can be devastating to your relationship. That's why Paul commanded the believers in Ephesus to "get rid of all bitterness, rage and anger, brawling and slander, along with every form of malice. Be kind and compassionate to one another, forgiving each other, just as in Christ God forgave you" (Eph. 4:31–32). Paul knew just how damaging unforgiveness and bitterness could be. He had seen it blow apart churches and blow up marriages. I have too. You can't afford to carry the burden of bitterness toward your spouse. You might as well be injecting poison into your veins.

Pray for a forgiving spirit. Pray for humility. Pray for the gift of brokenness. Ask God to reveal your own sins to you and to help you take your eyes off your spouse's sins. Pray for God to help you to see your spouse with his eyes—with love and compassion.

Pray also for the courage to confront the bitterness and unforgiveness in your marriage. Pray for the ability to have meaningful conversations about *why* the hurt is there in the first place. Ask God to help you to get counseling, to seek a mentoring couple, to talk to a pastor, or to do whatever is necessary to get the hurt out into the light.

I recently led a Bible study for a few couples. During one of the sessions, one of the wives shared that she was still hurt over a bad business decision her husband had made years before. They had never talked about it, and her anger was poisoning both her and their marriage. Her confession was a good first step toward their healing.

Bitterness is an all-too-common victor in Christian marriages. Pray that it won't have a place in yours.

Pray Big Prayer Starter

If you're currently angry or bitter toward your spouse, pray for God to pour out his favor on him or her. Your prayers will humble you and change your heart toward your spouse.

Busyness. Busyness is an insidious threat to marriage because it's so subtle. Couples who start out deeply in love and committed to each other can grow cold, calloused, and uncaring over the years, simply because they're too busy to cultivate a healthy relationship. Tragically and ironically, they are busy trying to work themselves into a "better" life.

How would you like to be remembered as the biblical character who was too busy for Jesus? For over two thousand years, that's the label that has stuck with Martha, the sister of Lazarus and Mary. While Jesus sat and instructed a crowd of eager listeners, including Mary, Martha busied herself with dinner preparations. Isn't that what many of us do in marriage? We rush around, fly from city to city, work late hours and weekends, spend evenings with clients, and pull all-nighters on projects, while the person of our dreams goes to sleep night after night in a half-empty bed.

Please don't fall prey to the trap of busyness. Nothing you are pursuing is worth damaging your marriage. Nothing. I once knew a very affluent couple who decided to build a massive house on a beautiful country lot outside of Austin. Actually, it was on two lots. They bought two houses, tore them both down, and built a huge mansion in their place. The house had every bell and whistle imaginable—a giant home theater, closets the size of most people's bedrooms, shower stalls with views of the hill country, a high-security panic room, a gated drive. The wife traveled the world finding just the right pieces for the home's finishing touches—an ancient rain gutter from Rome, crushed granite from Turkey, a unique piece of art from Brazil.

The couple spent over two years and several million dollars building the house. The husband worked full-time to pay their mortgages while the wife worked full-time overseeing the construction. They knew their marriage was taking a hit, but they figured the sacrifice would be worth it when they settled into their new, luxurious home.

When the house was finally finished, the couple even had a ceremony dedicating their home to God's glory. They toasted their home with expensive champagne and prayed for God's blessing on their new house. The wife cried. It was all quite beautiful.

Two months later, the wife asked her husband to move out. He was quickly replaced by another man, and the divorce was final a few months later. Now the wife is gone as well, and someone else owns their dream home.

Pray for God to protect you from the snare of busyness. Pray that time and intimacy with your spouse will always be a higher priority than busying yourself accumulating nice things. Ask God to make you content with what you have.

Pray Big Prayer Starter

Pray that next to being an obedient Christ-follower, cultivating a healthy marriage will be your most important priority.

Pornography. A church member called me recently, asking for advice. He had just discovered that his father, a long-time leader in his church, was addicted to pornography. The church member wanted to know how to help his father. I wish I could say that I was shocked by the story, but I wasn't.

With the advent of the Internet, a man's ability to access pornography has become frighteningly convenient. I say "a man's ability" because experience and statistics tell me that few women spend time Googling sexually explicit material. It is, almost exclusively, a man's sin. The consequences of the sin, however, are not limited to just the male users. Families, churches, businesses, government agencies, and political leaders have all felt the impact of America's growing addiction to Internet sex.

Recently in Austin, several Emergency Medical Service paramedics were fired after they were caught using city computers to access porn sites. Pornography—the objectification of women, the glorification of sex, and the entitlement mentality of the male libido—has become pervasive in our culture. America's preoccupation with sex closely resembles the histories of such failed cultures as the Greeks, the

141

Romans, and the cultures that dotted the landscape in the centuries before Christ—all of which no longer exist.

I have no doubt that the greatest threat to America's internal health and security is the redefining of our sexual DNA through the rapid growth of sexual deviance and the collective casting off of God's sexual standards. Many of my colleagues around the country share my conviction. The disciple Peter could just have easily been talking about our culture when he wrote, "Be self-controlled and alert. Your enemy the devil prowls around like a roaring lion looking for someone to devour" (1 Peter 5:8). Men are being devoured on a daily basis, and their own runaway appetites are killing them.

I need to be very clear here. I'm not saying that there aren't other serious temptations that married people face every day. We all know that there are. Rather, I am saying that Internet pornography, sexually oriented chat rooms, and websites that promote homosexuality, pedophilia, and other sexual deviations have taken a man's ability to saturate his mind with images of such perversions to an entirely new and devastating level. Romans 1:18–32 teaches in graphic language that when a nation disregards God's standards of sexuality, its own cultural destruction is never far behind. My fear is that we are seeing the frightening prophecies of this passage fulfilled before our very eyes.

Did you notice the instruction Peter gave to his readers before issuing his warning? "Be self-controlled." Sexual desire doesn't have to win the day in your life, your marriage, or our nation. Like any other God-given appetite, it can be disciplined and brought under control. So pray. Pray that God will protect your home from the influence of pornography. Pray that your sexual relationship will be healthy and gratifying for you and your spouse. Ask God to give you the discipline to rein in your rebellious appetites. Pray that you'll hate sin and any image, video, or scene that is dishonoring to God.

Pray Big Prayer Starter

Pray that Psalm 101:3 will be true for you and your spouse—*Lord, I will set no vile thing before my eyes.*

Fighting Back

The good news is that you don't have to sit back and wait for these temptations to come calling. You can go on the offensive and put a battle plan into action that will shore up and protect your marriage. That plan involves pinpoint praying. To help you get ready to take the battle to the enemy, you need to learn three important biblical principles.

Principle #1—The power of Jesus's blood. In Exodus 12:21–23, as part of the preparation for the Israelites' deliverance from the nation of Egypt, God instructed the leader of every home to spread the blood of a sacrificed lamb over the door frames of his house. In this first Passover, the blood of the lamb protected each firstborn inside the house from the sting of the death angel who visited Egypt on that terrible night. The blood over the house's door frames identified its occupants as the people of God.

The New Testament teaches that Jesus is the Lamb of God whose blood was shed once and for all for the sins of humankind. He was the ultimate Passover sacrifice. His blood has more power than any goat's, bull's, or lamb's. Jesus's blood paved the way for our access to God and covers all the sins of humanity.

When you pray for your marriage, pray that Jesus's blood will mark the door frames of your house. Ask that your home be clearly identified as one where people of God reside. Pray that Christ's blood will protect your home and your marriage from the onslaught of Satan.

Pray Big Prayer Starter

Pray that the power of Jesus's blood
will cover your home.
Ask God to mark you as his people.

Principle #2—Resisting the devil. A few years ago, Susie and our daughters took a self-defense class from a Tae Kwon Do instructor who attends our church. Before the instructor taught them any moves, kicks, or punches, she gave them a short talk. She basically said, "I want you to decide right now, today, that if you're ever attacked, you're going to fight back. You can't wait until you're surprised by a potential perp to decide what you're going to do. You have to make your plan of action long before the fight ever starts. Decide at this very moment that you will fight and resist. Never give in."

That's great advice, and it applies to fighting for our marriages as well. If you're in a Christian marriage, the question is not *if* you will be attacked but *when*. Temptation will come. Traps will be laid. Opportunities for sin will increase. In light of that, decide right now that you're going to fight. Know that Satan will attack you, and know that you can overcome him because of Jesus's power (see 1 John 4:4). Plan to resist, and then plan to prevail.

James 4:7 is your scriptural promise for resisting Satan: "Submit yourselves, then, to God. Resist the devil, and he will flee from you." When your marriage trials come, remind the devil that your marriage belongs to God. Tell him, in Jesus's name, that he has to leave you alone. Thank God every day for the victory you have over Satan in your marriage. Pray that you and your spouse will know how and when to resist the devil together in prayer.

Pray Big Prayer Starter

Ask God to rebuke the devil on behalf of your
family (see Jude 9). Pray that he'll defend you
from Satan's evil ways. Ask for the boldness and
faith to resist Satan in Jesus's holy name.

Principle #3—Walking and praying. There is a powerful
promise that God gives to the Israelites' new spiritual leader,
Joshua, on the eve of their invasion of the Promised Land:
"I will give you every place where you set your foot, as I
promised Moses" (Josh. 1:3). In other words, "Wherever you
walk, wherever the soles of your feet tread, claim it for me,
and I'll give it to you." I've prayed this verse for my family
and put it into practice on countless occasions.

Recently I was awakened in the middle of the night by
our home's alarm system. Shaking off the fog of sleep, I
did a quick mental inventory of reasons our alarm might
be sounding. The most common culprit is my college-age
son, who frequently comes in long after we've gone to bed.
However, he was away at school. I couldn't think of another
good reason for our alarm to be sounding at three in the
morning. So I got out of bed, reset the alarm, and began to
look around our house.

Every door was securely locked, every window tightly
closed. That was good news, but it seemed strange. Our
alarm system has never sounded without a reason. Something always triggers it. But on this occasion, I couldn't find
the source. Fear began to play tricks on my mind. *Is someone
in the house? Is someone outside trying to break in? Am I
going to have to fight to protect my family? Will they be safe?*
I suddenly found myself gripped by a sense of dread.

Then, by God's grace, my spiritual instincts kicked in. I
began to walk around my house, claiming Joshua 1:3. I asked
the Lord to name our house as his and to protect every inch my
feet walked. I went into my daughters' bedrooms and prayed

over them. I prayed with Susie. I asked God to protect our home and to cover it with Jesus's blood. I rebuked Satan in Jesus's name and told him he had no authority in my home.

A few weeks later, we learned that a team of thieves had been working our neighborhood. They were breaking into homes at night, tying up the occupants, and ransacking the houses. I don't know if they triggered our alarm that night, but I do know that God used the occasion to remind me to regularly walk my house and pray.

There is a spiritual thief who is always looking for a way into your home (see John 10:10). Pray for protection against him.

Pray Big Prayer Starter

Walk your house and pray for a supernatural barrier of protection to be placed around it. Ask God to make every square inch of it holy. Remind Satan, in Jesus's name, that it is God's property, and ask God to make it free from Satan's evil ways.

Pray Big Today

The combination of praying that Jesus's blood will cover your home, resisting the devil in Jesus's name, and walking and praying around your house is a potent trifecta for those who want to anoint their marriage in prayer. Those three pinpoint prayers will help you and your spouse be better equipped to prevail over the marriage temptations that inevitably will come. Here are some other suggestions:

- Pray Scripture for your house. Find verses that talk about the kind of home you want to have and pray them regularly.

146

- Pray over the potential sources of temptation in your house. Pray over your television and computer. Pray also in your dining room, living room, and bedrooms. Ask God to make them holy.
- Pray for your spouse to be holy ground. Ask God to be fully enthroned and for his glory to be fully manifested in your spouse's life.
- Pray that you and your spouse will be quick to forgive. Ask God to protect you from any bitterness or unforgiveness that might develop between the two of you.
- Pray for appropriate pacing in your lives. Ask God to help you both to manage your time well and to be ruthless about protecting your time together.
- Pray against pornography. Pray that it won't work its way into your home or become a stronghold in either of your lives.
- Pray that you'll both be wise and discerning when dealing with people of the opposite sex. Pray that you will quickly run from any sort of sexual temptation or relational blurred lines.

Verses to Pray for Your Marriage's Protection

- Ephesians 4:26–27: *Father, help us learn how to process our anger and disagreements appropriately. I pray that we won't leave a place for Satan to establish a stronghold.*
- Hosea 2:6: *Holy God, please place a hedge of thorns around our marriage so that we will not be tempted to wander into sin.*
- Job 1:10: *Lord, please establish a hedge of protection around our marriage so that Satan might not harm us.*

147

A Marriage Pinpoint Prayer

Holy God, I ask you to protect my marriage. I am fully aware of the battle we're fighting. I know Satan wants to destroy my marriage. I ask you to rebuke him. Place your holy covering on my marriage. Help my spouse and me to always be humble and sensitive to the promptings of your Holy Spirit. Teach us to recognize temptation and to run away from it. Help us to hate sin and to always resist the devil in Jesus's name. Cover us with your holy blood and make our marriage holy ground. I pray this in Jesus's name. Amen.

11

PRAYING FOR YOUR
MARRIAGE MISSION

BRANDON PARKER IS a handsome, athletic young man
with a pitching arm that could easily be mistaken for a
cannon. When God was handing out talent, he gave an extra
dosage of unction to Brandon's right arm, and it didn't take
professional baseball scouts long to notice. Drafted out of
college, Brandon began a successful career pitching for both
major- and independent-league baseball teams. A boy from
a small town in Mississippi, Brandon was living his dream.
He was getting paid to play ball.

But there is more to Brandon than baseball. He is a mighty
man of God who is passionately in love with Christ. He grew
up in church and ended up falling in love with his pastor's
youngest daughter—an equally passionate Christian and
gifted worship leader named Amber. Amber's father gave
Brandon permission to marry his daughter, and the couple
planned to wed in their home church, New Life Christian

Church, in Pass Christian, Mississippi. The date was set for the fall of 2005. Amber and Brandon couldn't have been more blessed—they were going to be married, they were both godly young people, and they would get to be a part of the exciting world of professional baseball.

And then Hurricane Katrina struck. Pass Christian, Mississippi, took a direct hit from Katrina. The beautiful little village, located just east of Gulfport, was hit by 180-mile-per-hour winds and swamped by a thirty-foot tidal wave. Everything was devastated. Amber and Brandon, along with the rest of their family and the few remaining Pass Christian residents, woke up on August 30, 2005, to a new normal. The life, dreams, and homes they loved were gone. Much of the physical infrastructure of what was Pass Christian now lay out in the bay, in what is believed to be a three-mile-wide debris field hidden below the water's surface.

Amber and Brandon were immediately caught up in the storm after the storm. They moved into a hand-to-mouth, day-to-day, tragedy-after-tragedy, miracle-after-miracle existence that would last the better part of a year. New Life Christian Church, because of its location and extra acreage, became a distribution center for the thousands of storm survivors and relief workers who poured into the area. Amber and Brandon, along with countless others, worked long days and nights trying to rebuild the lives, homes, businesses, and churches that had been stolen by the storm. The two were married, took a brief honeymoon, and got back to work.

Then the scouts came calling again. Brandon, who had been out of baseball for a year, was invited to play for a professional-league team in Jackson, Mississippi. The scouts offered Brandon more than just the opportunity to play ball professionally; they offered him and Amber a way out. The move to Jackson and the distraction of a professional career would free them from having to wake up every day to the unending struggle their lives had become. Who would blame them for taking the money, the job security, the fun and ease, and running like crazy?

But they didn't take the offer. Brandon turned it down and decided to commit at least a year to his church and his pastor/father-in-law. He pledged himself to giving his best efforts to rebuilding Pass Christian and building Jesus's kingdom in the midst of it. He and Amber dedicated their marriage to Christ's cause and his glory. Whatever their future held, they were in it together with Jesus. They spent the next two years living in FEMA and/or donated trailers, working for their church for little or no pay, testifying to the goodness of God, and impacting the lives of people from all over the country—mine included.

What's the point of your marriage? Why does it exist? Why did God bring you and your spouse together? Was it just to make you happy? Was it to procreate and to help keep the earth well populated? Or was it for more than that?

Pray Big Prayer Starter

Ask God to use your marriage to touch others' lives.

Till Death or Unhappiness Do Us Part

Many people get married for the wrong reasons. Christians are no exception. They go to the altar with another person in hopes of finding some higher level of fulfillment. That is one of the reasons the divorce rate in the United States is so high—we marry for the wrong reasons and ask marriage to give us something it can't.

Have you stopped to think about why you got married or what you ultimately hope to accomplish in your marriage?

Here are some common statements that sum up many couples' marriage goals:

- *We just want to be happy.* This isn't a good reason to get married. Marriage is hard work and can lead people through incredibly difficult seasons. If happiness is the goal, marriage can be a big disappointment.
- *We want to have sex and not feel guilty about it.* Couples who know that sex before marriage is wrong but can't control themselves often name this as a reason to get married. As we learned in chapter 5, sexual intimacy may be the *lowest* level of relational intimacy—not a good enough reason to marry.
- *We want to live comfortably and retire well.* This is a subtle goal of a number of marriages. Many spouses are prepared to work long, hard years to accumulate nice things, secure themselves in retirement, and even provide for their children and grandchildren. While there is nothing inherently wrong with these motives, they are not particularly noble marriage goals.
- *We want to have a meaningful, lifelong partnership.* This is a good marriage desire and something that God wants for your marriage, but it is still very self-oriented. God wants you to enjoy decades of profound levels of relational intimacy, but he wants you to do so against the backdrop of a marriage purpose that is bigger than you both.

It's All About . . . Others

Have you ever thought that God might have a larger, more kingdom-oriented purpose for your marriage? Have you ever prayed for a vision for your marriage? I don't mean a vision of what God wants to do for *you* through your marriage. I'm talking about what God wants to do for *others* through your marriage. I'm talking about your marriage mission.

Earlier in the book I introduced you to Priscilla and Aquila, a committed Christian couple who worked closely with the apostle Paul. Here is Luke's summary of how they initially met Paul: "Paul left Athens and went to Corinth. There he met a Jew named Aquila, a native of Pontus, who had recently come from Italy with his wife Priscilla, because Claudius had ordered all the Jews to leave Rome. Paul went to see them, and because he was a tentmaker as they were, he stayed and worked with them" (Acts 18:1–3). We've already noted that this Christian couple probably had an intimate marriage relationship because they were both quite spiritually mature. But I want you to think about another aspect of their marriage that we didn't consider earlier: their ministry.

Priscilla and Aquila were a ministry-minded couple. Though they served as professional tentmakers, their real passion was ministry. They were close friends and ministry allies with Paul, as well as being leaders of a house church in Corinth (see 1 Cor. 16:19). Their ministry took on a role and mission that far exceeded their own personal wants and needs. They had an others-centered, high-impact marriage that added an element of adventure and mission to their relationship. They had the thrill of knowing that God was using them to expand his kingdom and bless the lives of others, not just as individual Christ-followers but also as a couple.

How would your marriage be different if you knew that you and your spouse were being used to funnel God's blessings to others? How might your conversations or arguments, spending habits, vacation discussions, and retirement plans change if you both felt compelled to fulfill your marriage's calling? Having a marriage mission adds even more depth to the spiritual and emotional intimacy we discussed in previous chapters. Twice in Matthew, Jesus taught that if we wanted to find true life, we had to lose ours (see Matt. 10:39 and 16:25). The same is true for marriage. If you want your marriage to have profound meaning, then start using it for the benefit of others.

Pray Big Prayer Starter

Pray for a vision of how God wants to use you and your spouse to serve others.

The Benefits of Having a Marriage Mission

Two seven-year-olds who don't know each other are swinging side by side on a playground swing set. As each of the children's respective arcs grows higher, they appear to be swinging in rhythm. The high points at the beginning and end of each arc are identical. It looks as if the kids are swinging together, pushed along by the same unseen hand. The kids, thrilled by their mutual collaboration, begin to giggle and shout back and forth as they continue their swinging duet. When they're finished, they jump off the swings together and run off to play a new game, now as friends.

Believe it or not, that playful interaction actually has a technical name: *interactional synchrony*. Interactional synchrony is the intentional, cooperative movement by more than one person. It can be expressed in something as simple as a stimulating conversation or kids swinging legs together while sitting side by side on a picnic table. Interactional synchrony is at work in the group dynamics of a rowing team, a marching band, or a choreographed dance. Psychologists, without fully understanding why, believe that there is a powerful emotional pull between humans who choose to cooperate on various levels. And as you might expect, the higher the level of relational interaction, the higher the level of emotional bonding that occurs.

I believe the highest level of interactional synchrony is in a marriage mission. What could be more exciting, more invigorating, and more emotionally bonding than a Christian man and woman working together through marriage to benefit the lives of others? Against the backdrop of a culture that says marriage is all about getting *your* needs met, couples who choose to use marriage to serve others really do stand out as lights in a dark world. Beyond that, a couple's own level of joy and fulfillment in marriage will typically increase as they learn to use their corporate strengths for God's kingdom. Let's look briefly at some of the benefits of having a mutual marriage mission.

Having a marriage mission helps a couple take their eyes off themselves. I know many Christian couples today, couples with significant kingdom potential, who are totally wrapped up in themselves. Their whole married lives revolve around their next home, their next vacation, their kids' education, their social functions, their next date with a personal trainer, and their portfolio. Please note that I am not saying these things are inherently wrong. I am saying that they make for woefully inadequate marriage missions. Surely we can find better uses for our marriage synchronism.

On the other hand, I know many other Christian couples who have leveraged their marriage for serious kingdom purposes, and every day they see the fruit of their labors. Not only do they have the joy of seeing God use them, but they know the relational thrill and intimacy that come only when they've combined efforts for something holy. Couples who have a kingdom marriage mission simply have more to live for than those who don't.

Having a marriage mission gives you even more reason to fight for your marriage. Marriage is hard. We all know that. Even the strongest marriages go through seasons of testing and difficulty. Without the glue of the Holy Spirit and a commitment to covenant love in marriage, couples can all too easily decide that their marriage assignment is just too difficult.

A Christian counselor told me recently that she is seeing an "epidemic" of separations and divorces among Christian couples. The most tragic part is that the couples have very little reason to end the marriage. There has been no infidelity or abuse of any kind. Rather, many couples are choosing to quit their marriages these days simply because they're not happy, or not happy enough.

Having a marriage mission gives you compelling reasons not just to stay married but to have a healthy marriage. A husband and wife who are mentoring young married couples, leading a Bible study for unchurched people, serving in leadership roles in their church, spending time in short-term missions, giving significant amounts of money to ministries, working with troubled youth, or leading a prayer ministry will understand the impact if their marriage fails. Couples with marriage missions know how high the stakes are. They are fighting for more than just their own marriage. They are fighting for all the lives they impact currently and might impact in the future. Susie and I both feel motivated to keep our marriage strong and healthy, not just for our sake and the sake of our children, but also for the sake of the many lives God has given us the opportunity to impact. Letting our marriage fail would be one of the most selfish things we could do.

Having a marriage mission humbles you and drives you to prayer. In Acts 1, Luke records Jesus's final instructions to his disciples: "You will receive power when the Holy Spirit comes on you; and you will be my witnesses in Jerusalem, and in all Judea and Samaria, and to the ends of the earth" (Acts 1:8). Talk about a bold mission! Basically, Jesus told the disciples that even though they were outlaws, undermanned, outgunned, and fewer than 150 in number, they would take his message around the world. Jesus's Great Commission to his disciples had its desired effect—it humbled them and drove them to their knees in prayer. Acts 1:14 tells us, "They all joined together constantly in prayer." That's what a massive kingdom mission does—it takes your breath away, humbles you, and makes you seek God.

Do you want to keep your marriage in the proper perspective? Do you want to stay focused on the big picture of God's kingdom and off the tiny details of your personal wants and needs? Do you want to see your spouse as a kingdom ally and not a relational foe? Then seek a marriage mission. Attach your marriage to a purpose that's so large, so majestic, and so humanly impossible that it humbles you and your spouse before God, drives you to prayer, and gives you something beyond yourselves to live for.

Pray Big Prayer Starter

Ask God to show you a group of people, a part of the world, or an area of life that you and your spouse are both passionate about and could impact together. Then ask him to lead you to a ministry opportunity in that area.

The Beauty of a Marriage Mission

There is no magic formula for finding a kingdom assignment for your marriage. All it takes is two mutually submitted believers who want their marriage to be about more than their own happiness. Mix in their willingness to be used by

God, and you've got a great recipe for discovering a marriage mission. Couples whose marriages have a higher purpose and calling will tell you their greatest joys in marriage come in having an others-centered orientation. Consider the following examples.

Ryan and Courtney Nowakowski. They love Jesus, are very involved in church, and are high-level black belts in Tae Kwon Do. I learned a long time ago never to accuse Courtney of hitting like a girl. Her "girl" punch can put me on the ground. Beyond that, her husband knows approximately fifteen ways to end my life in two seconds or less with his bare hands and feet. I'm always on my best behavior when the Nowakowskis are around.

The Nowakowskis own a Tae Kwon Do academy where they help people of all ages get in shape, gain personal discipline and inner strength, and learn how to respect authority. They're highly respected and greatly loved by their clientele.

Courtney and Ryan have also fallen in love with missions. They've spent many a week in the dead heat of summer helping build houses in incredibly impoverished parts of Mexico. They were highly involved in our church's Hurricane Katrina relief efforts. And recently, when a teen in our church ran away from a troubled home situation, guess who he ended up calling? The Nowakowskis. Their marriage has taken on a major serving component that I doubt either one of them saw coming.

Ryan and Courtney's marriage mission has given them even more reason to work and pray for their marriage. They are humbled by what God is doing in them and thrilled that their relationship can have a kingdom-sized outlet.

Alan and Tina Nagel. Alan and Tina are one of the godliest couples I know. Their multidecade marriage has touched countless lives. Alan walked away from a lucrative, family-owned dairy business to go on staff with Campus Crusade for Christ. He and Tina traded the comfort and "security" that money can bring for the faith-based life of raising support for their income. For over thirty years the Nagels have made their marriage mission one of discipling believers and sharing Christ with unbelievers.

Alan and Tina's marriage mission has a life of its own. Mention the Nagels in certain settings in Austin, or even around the world, and people immediately think of a couple whose marriage is fully yielded to Christ. Alan and Tina have prayed for, mentored, encouraged, instructed, rebuked, and led people in kingdom business all over the world. Their ministry impacts Christian leaders and the people those leaders serve.

The Nagels would be the first to tell you that their marriage isn't perfect. But it's used for Christ's purposes, by helping others see his kingdom. Alan and Tina would also tell you that they have never regretted walking away from the potential wealth of the dairy business. What they have seen and done together in God's kingdom far outweighs any earthly treasure.

Rick and Stephanie Reynolds. Rick and Stephanie's marriage is all about helping other marriages. Rick is a Christian counselor who specializes in working with couples in crisis. His job requires many long days, nights, and even weekends, serving couples whose relationships are on the brink of total failure. Stephanie is an active partner in Rick's ministry. Together they serve couples who are facing challenges that can quickly end a marriage.

Several times a year, Rick and Stephanie spend the weekend with a few other couples in a house by a lake outside of Austin. They call the weekend an EMS (Emergency Marriage Services) weekend. The pain, intensity, spiritual warfare, and emotional exhaustion these weekends produce is difficult to comprehend, yet Rick and Stephanie show no sign of backing off.

Their marriage mission is to help save other marriages. They have leveraged the best of their time, resources, and years left on earth to fight for families. Their marriage calling is certainly not an easy one, but it's one they would never leave. They've seen too many lives changed, seen too many marriages saved, and found way too much joy to ever consider doing something else.

John and Helen Boyd. When I was fifteen years old, I was a competitive water-skier and was not attending church. My training and travel schedule typically took me away from church on weekends. I soon came to think that church wasn't cool enough for me anyway. One night my tenth grade Sunday school teacher, John Boyd, and a few kids from church came to visit me at home. I had been around church enough to know that only the really "bad" kids got these surprise visits. I was offended and even embarrassed that I had become one of those kids. I was so embarrassed, in fact, that I turned off the front porch light and acted like I wasn't home.

The next Sunday I went to church and confronted Mr. Boyd. I told him that I wasn't a bad kid who needed visiting. His answer totally disarmed me. He simply responded that he and the kids from church loved me, missed me, and wanted me to know that I was welcome in their class. That was thirty years ago, and I've been going to church ever since.

John and Helen are a godly Christian couple whose marriage mission is to serve teenagers. There are very few perks for getting up early on Sunday and trying to rouse a bunch of sleepy tenth graders into being interested in spiritual things. But that's exactly what the Boyds did for over twenty-five years. In some cases, they've not really been aware of their impact. But their impact is clear in my case. I am a Christian, husband, father, pastor, and author who would not have started going back to church, recommitted my life to Christ, felt called to ministry, or met my wife at church if it wasn't for the Boyds' love, prayers, concern, and investment. I'm one of countless living examples of the impact of their marriage mission.

Pray Big Today

I recently talked to my friends Amber and Brandon Parker in Mississippi. They were driving to Houston (seven hours one way) to pray with a woman in the hospital who was battling late-stage cancer. The woman's daughter was in their youth group, and they felt led to travel to Houston, lay hands on the woman, and ask God to heal her. After I hung up, I thought again about Brandon and Amber's commitment to Christ. Here was this young married couple who could have been doing so many other things with their time, but instead they chose to drive fourteen hours round-trip to spend a few minutes interceding for an ailing woman. I remember thinking, *I want to be that radical for Christ. I want my marriage to have that much impact for God's kingdom. I want to know the kind of intimacy that comes from being used by God in marriage.*

Do you want to create an avenue for God to heat up your spiritual intimacy? Look for ways to minister together as a couple. Pray for opportunities to work hard, sweat, invest, and sacrifice together on behalf of someone else. Ask God to give you both a servant's heart and an others-centered mind-set. Ask God to make your marriage a blessing to others. Pray for a marriage mission. The experiences you'll share as a result will knit your souls together in a way that nothing else can.

Verses to Pray for Your Marriage Mission

- 2 Thessalonians 1:11–12: *Father, please make us worthy of your calling on our marriage, that by your power we may fulfill every good purpose and every act prompted by our faith. I ask this so that the name of our Lord Jesus may be glorified in us, and us in him, according to the grace of God and the Lord Jesus Christ.*

- Colossians 1:10–11: *Father, please equip us to live a life worthy of your name, and help us to please you in every way. Help us to bear fruit in every good work, grow in the knowledge of who you are, and be strengthened with all power according to your glorious might, so that we may have endurance and patience in the ministry you have given us.*

- John 15:5, 8: *Holy Lord, show us how to abide in you as a couple so that we can bear much fruit and glorify your name.*

A Marriage Pinpoint Prayer[1]

Holy Father, we commit our marriage to you. We ask you to give us a vision and calling that go way beyond us. Equip us to love, minister to, and serve others through the avenue of our marriage relationship. Give us a heart for people who need you. Show us how we can best leverage our time, resources, and skills for your kingdom. We pray that you would take our marriage and consider it fully yours. Use us as you please for your kingdom. We ask this in Jesus's name. Amen.

Appendix

A Month of Pinpoint Prayers for Your Marriage

BELOW ARE THIRTY-ONE pinpoint prayers for your marriage. I believe that you'll find each to be biblical, specific, and relevant. Read through these prayers and know that God will answer them. As you pray them for your marriage, he will honor you.

In each day's entry, you'll find a verse followed by a prayer written from it. I've deliberately chosen short, easy-to-learn verses. Don't rush through them. Try to memorize each verse and meditate on it. As you master its concepts, you'll be able to pray it with more confidence and passion. Pray big!

Day 1

Verse: "'For this reason a man will leave his father and mother and be united to his wife, and the two will become one flesh.' So they are no longer two, but one. Therefore what God has joined together, let man not separate" (Mark 10:7–9).

Prayer: *Holy God and Creator, we acknowledge your eternal purpose for our marriage. Help us to fully cleave to each other and to become one flesh. Make us one, O Lord, and bind us together so that nothing will ever come between us.*

Day 2

Verse: "Seek first his kingdom and his righteousness, and all these things will be given to you as well" (Matt. 6:33).

Prayer: *Father, help us as a couple to prioritize your kingdom and your righteousness in our marriage. As we do, please provide for all of our needs.*

Day 3

Verse: "I will give them singleness of heart and action, so that they will always fear me for their own good and the good of their children after them" (Jer. 32:39).

Prayer: *Mighty God, please give my spouse and me singleness of heart and action. Give us one heart in our marriage. Help us to always honor you, for our own good and for the benefit of our children.*

Day 4

Verse: "Our Father in heaven, hallowed be your name" (Matt. 6:9).

Prayer: *Dear God, you are holy. Please let your name be praised and honored by our marriage relationship.*

Day 5

Verse: "Your kingdom come, your will be done on earth as it is in heaven" (Matt. 6:10).

Prayer: *Holy Father, we pray that you will build your kingdom in our marriage. We also pray that your will would be accomplished in our marriage as quickly and immediately as it is in heaven.*

Day 6

Verse: "Give us today our daily bread" (Matt. 6:11).

Prayer: *Holy God, you are the God who provides. We ask you to meet our needs today and to help us to be content with what we have.*

Day 7

Verse: "Forgive us our debts, as we also have forgiven our debtors" (Matt. 6:12).

Prayer: *Dear Jesus, you died to grant us God's forgiveness. Please help us to grant immediate forgiveness to each other.*

Day 8

Verse: "And lead us not into temptation, but deliver us from the evil one" (Matt. 6:13).

Prayer: *Mighty God, we seek your protection. Keep us free from temptation and protect us from Satan's evil schemes.*

Day 9

Verse: "A good name is more desirable than great riches; to be esteemed is better than silver or gold" (Prov. 22:1).

Prayer: *Precious Father, we are your people. Give our family a good name. We want to honor you more than we want to have silver, gold, or great riches.*

Day 10

Verse: "As God's chosen people, holy and dearly loved, clothe yourselves with compassion, kindness, humility, gentleness and patience" (Col. 3:12).

Prayer: *Father, we are your holy people. Help us in this marriage to always be clothed with compassion, kindness, humility, gentleness, and patience.*

Day 11

Verse: "Now, my God, may your eyes be open and your ears attentive to the prayers offered in this place" (2 Chron. 6:40).

Prayer: *Mighty Lord, please anoint our home with your holy presence. Please hear and answer the prayers we offer here. Grant us your favor as your holy people.*

Day 12

Verse: "He is like a tree planted by streams of water, which yields its fruit in season and whose leaf does not wither. Whatever he does prospers" (Ps. 1:3).

Prayer: *Father, plant our marriage deeply in your Word. Cause us to be fruitful, and let all we do prosper for your glory.*

Day 13

Verse: "Do not let any unwholesome talk come out of your mouths, but only what is helpful for building others up according to their needs, that it may benefit those who listen" (Eph. 4:29).

Prayer: *Precious Father, guard and guide the way we speak to each other in our marriage. Help us to never speak hateful or hurtful words to each other. Teach us instead to speak only loving and affirming words.*

Day 14

Verse: "Marriage should be honored by all, and the marriage bed kept pure, for God will judge the adulterer and all the sexually immoral" (Heb. 13:4).

Prayer: *Father, help us to honor your institution of marriage. Keep our marriage pure and free from adultery and all sexual immorality.*

Day 15

Verse: "In the same way, let your light shine before men, that they may see your good deeds and praise your Father in heaven" (Matt. 5:16).

Prayer: *Lord God, make our marriage a bright light for you. Let the good works of our marriage bring praise to your awesome name.*

Day 16

Verse: "By this all men will know that you are my disciples, if you love one another" (John 13:35).

Prayer: *Mighty Savior, let the profound love in our marriage show all who know us that we are your disciples and that we have a Christ-honoring relationship.*

Day 17

Verse: "May those who hope in you not be disgraced because of me, O Lord, the LORD Almighty; may those who seek you not be put to shame because of me, O God of Israel" (Ps. 69:6).

Prayer: *Holy God, let our marriage always glorify and honor your name. Make yourself famous in us. We pray that your people would never have reason to be ashamed or embarrassed because of anything in our marriage.*

Day 18

Verse: "Finally, brothers, whatever is true, whatever is noble, whatever is right, whatever is pure, whatever is lovely, whatever is admirable—if anything is excellent or praiseworthy—think about such things" (Phil. 4:8).

Prayer: *Holy God, make our home holy. Help us as a couple to reflect on and talk about things that are pure, right, holy, just, and worthy of your holy name.*

Day 19

Verse: "Since, then, you have been raised with Christ, set your hearts on things above, where Christ is seated at the right hand of God. Set your minds on things above, not on earthly things" (Col. 3:1–2).

Prayer: *Dear Jesus, our eyes and hearts are set on you. Please give us a marriage vision for things eternal—things that are part of your kingdom—and not for things of the earth.*

Day 20

Verse: "Love the LORD your God with all your heart and with all your soul and with all your strength" (Deut. 6:5).

Prayer: *Lord, you are our God. We will love you as a family with all of our heart, soul, and strength.*

Day 21

Verse: "And we know that in all things God works for the good of those who love him, who have been called according to his purpose" (Rom. 8:28).

Prayer: *Holy Father, because we are called by your name and purpose, we pray that you will cause all things in our marriage— joy and sadness, blessing and pain, victory and defeat—to work together for good.*

Day 22

Verse: "Whether you turn to the right or to the left, your ears will hear a voice behind you, saying, 'This is the way; walk in it'" (Isa. 30:21).

Prayer: *Holy Father, please guide our decision making. As we go through our lives together, help us to be attentive and obedient to your voice.*

Day 23

Verse: "Everyone who hears these words of mine and puts them into practice is like a wise man who built his house on the rock" (Matt. 7:24).

Prayer: *Holy God, make us wise. Help us to build our marriage on the unshakable foundation of your Word.*

Day 24

Verse: " 'For I know the plans I have for you,' declares the LORD, 'plans to prosper you and not to harm you, plans to give you hope and a future' " (Jer. 29:11).

Prayer: *Holy Father, thank you for leading and guiding us in marriage. Please fulfill your great plans for us, giving us hope and a future.*

Day 25

Verse: "Just as you excel in everything—in faith, in speech, in knowledge, in complete earnestness and in your love for us—see that you also excel in this grace of giving" (2 Cor. 8:7).

Prayer: *Father God, let our marriage be excellent in the things that matter. Teach us to excel in our faith, in Christ-honoring speech, in knowledge of your ways, in our passion for you, and in the blessed privilege of giving to others.*

Day 26

Verse: "The husband should fulfill his marital duty to his wife, and likewise the wife to her husband. The wife's body does not belong to her alone but also to her husband. In the same way, the husband's body does not belong to him alone but also to his wife" (1 Cor. 7:3–4).

Prayer: *Lord God, your Word teaches that our bodies belong to you first and then to each other. Help us to satisfy each other and honor you in our sexual relationship.*

Day 27

Verse: "The fruit of the Spirit is love, joy, peace, patience, kindness, goodness, faithfulness, gentleness and self-control. Against such things there is no law" (Gal. 5:22–23).

Prayer: *Father, may the sweet fruit of your Holy Spirit—love, joy, peace, patience, kindness, goodness, faithfulness, gentleness, and self-control—be manifested for your glory in our marriage.*

Day 28

Verse: "The love of money is a root of all kinds of evil. Some people, eager for money, have wandered from the faith and pierced themselves with many griefs" (1 Tim. 6:10).

Prayer: *Lord God, we know that you are the source of all that we have. We understand that the pursuit of money and material gain can kill our faith and destroy our marriage. Please protect us from the love of money. Help us to always keep it in proper perspective.*

Day 29

Verse: "Unless the LORD builds the house, its builders labor in vain. Unless the LORD watches over the city, the watchmen stand guard in vain" (Ps. 127:1).

Prayer: *Lord God, our marriage belongs to you. Please be its chief architect and builder. Protect it from our own sins and vanities. Watch over our marriage and protect our home.*

Day 30

Verse: " 'In your anger do not sin': Do not let the sun go down while you are still angry, and do not give the devil a foothold" (Eph. 4:26–27).

Prayer: *Dear Jesus, teach us to have appropriate and healthy anger. Help us to not let our anger toward each other simmer or grow into bitterness. Protect us from satanic strongholds that could develop from our unforgiveness.*

Day 31

Verse: "The LORD bless you and keep you; the LORD make his face shine upon you and be gracious to you; the LORD turn his face toward you and give you peace" (Num. 6:24–26).

Prayer: *Lord God, we humbly seek your blessing, favor, anointing, and protection on our marriage. Smile on us and be gracious to us, according to your Word. Watch over us and give us peace.*

NOTES

Chapter 1: Dearly Beloved . . . Pray!

1. Sam Roberts, "To Be Married Means to Be Outnumbered," *New York Times*, October 15, 2006, http://www.nytimes.com/2006/10/15/us/15census .html?_r=1&oref=slogin.

Chapter 2: Big, Hairy, Audacious Prayers and Your Marriage

1. Will Davis Jr., *Pray Big* (Grand Rapids: Revell, 2007).

2. See B. A. Robinson, "U.S. Divorce Rates for Various Faith Groups, Age Groups, and Geographic Areas," Religioustolerance.org, April 27, 2000, http://www.religioustolerance.org/chr_dira.htm; and The Barna Group, "Born Again Christians Just As Likely to Divorce As Are Non-Christians," September 8, 2004, http://www.barna.org/FlexPage.aspx?Page=BarnaUpdate&BarnaUpdate ID=170.

3. See Catholic Marriage Care Service, "Couple Prayer," March 2007, http://www.accord.ie/staying_married/couple_prayer; and Michael Smalley, "Do You Know the Divorce Rate of Couples Who Pray Together?" Gosmalley.com, November 26, 2006, http://www.crashintolove.com/2006/11/26/do-you-know-the-divorce-rate-of-couples-who-pray-together.

Chapter 5: Praying for Spiritual Intimacy

1. Throughout the book, I use the word *soul* to speak of the God-given, eternal spirit that dwells within each human. It is the breath of life that God breathed into humans at creation. While *spirit* may be a more accurate term, I chose *soul* because it fits better in a relational context.

2. I wish I could take credit for the wonderful phrase "the lopsided favor of God," but I can't. Thanks to my creative and inspiring wife, Susie, for her potent description of God's goodness.

Chapter 7: How to Pray for Your Husband

1. "Wife Who Fought Mountain Lion: I'm No Hero," ABC News, January 8, 2007, http://abcnews.go.com/GMA/story?id=2829689&CMP=OTC-RSSFeeds0312.

Chapter 8: How to Pray for Your Wife

1. Andrée Seu, "Beauty at Any Price," *World Magazine*, May 7, 2005, 51.

Chapter 11: Praying for Your Marriage Mission

1. Regularly pray this prayer with your spouse, on your knees.

Will Davis Jr. is the founding and senior pastor of Austin Christian Fellowship in Austin, Texas. Will and his wife, Susie, have three children.

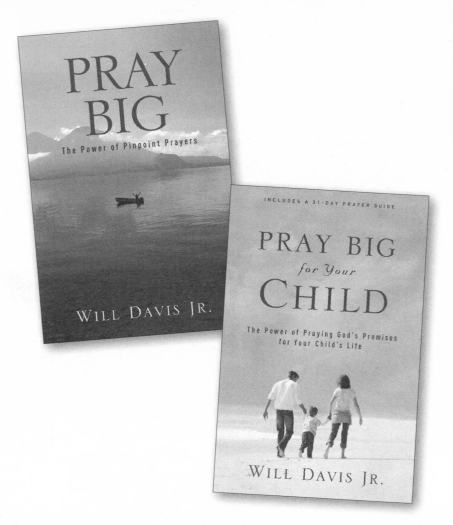